TWENTIETH-CENTURY
WOMEN SCIENTISTS

Global Profiles

TWENTIETH-CENTURY WOMEN SCIENTISTS

Lisa Yount

 Facts On File®

AN INFOBASE HOLDINGS COMPANY

Library of Congress Cataloging-in-Publication Data

Yount, Lisa
    Twentieth-century women scientists / Lisa Yount.
        p. cm. — (Global profiles)
    Includes bibliographical references and index.
    Summary: Includes biographies of ten women who have made significant contributions to modern science, including Barbara McClintock, Katsuko Saruhashi, E. Margaret Burbidge, and Lydia Phindile Makhubu.
    ISBN 0-8160-3173-8 (alk. paper)
    1. Women scientists—Biography—Juvenile literature. 2. Women in science—History—20th century—Juvenile literature. [1. Scientists. 2. Women in science—History. 3. Women—Biography.] I. Series.
Q141.Y69 1995
509.2'2—dc20
[B]   95-10888

Facts On File books are available at special discounts when purchased in bulk quantities for businesses, associations, institutions or sales promotions. Please call our Special Sales Department in New York at 212/967-8800 or 800/322-8755.

Text design by Catherine Rincon Hyman
Cover design by Nora Wertz

This book is printed on acid-free paper.
Printed in the United States of America.

MP FOF 10 9 8 7 6 5 4 3 2 1

Contents

Acknowledgments

I would like to thank Margaret Burbidge, Katsuko Saruhashi, R. Rajalakshmi, and Biruté Galdikas for patiently answering my questions about their lives and work. Thanks also to Sister Anita C. Smith for providing information about Lydia Makhubu and to William Harms for providing information about Aslihan Yener. And, finally, thanks to members of the Women's History Network for providing many helpful suggestions about possible women to include in the book; to Kat MacFarlane, for her usual excellent illustrations and diagrams; and to Harry Henderson, invaluable for technical support and everything else, including sending or attempting to send endless faxes to far-flung parts of the world.

"Science will . . . [try], by obeying the
law of Humanity,
to extend the frontiers of Life."

—Louis Pasteur

"Women have a great
responsibility . . . to try . . . to prevent
another war. I hope . . . that we will be able to
use this great [atomic] energy . . .
for peaceful work."

—Lise Meitner

Introduction

It could be argued that the discrimination and discouragement that most women scientists have faced in the 20th century did them a favor.

Great scientists, like great achievers in other fields, need to be supremely self-confident and determined. They frequently propose ideas that are just the opposite of what other scientists think. If experimental evidence supports their ideas, they must be willing to stick with those ideas in the face of criticism, feeling assured that time will prove them right. If no one will work with them, they must be able to work alone. They must also be imaginative and flexible. As Margaret Burbidge has written, "If frustrated in one's endeavor by a stone wall or any kind of blockage, one must find a way around—another route toward one's goal."

The women scientists profiled in this book had plenty of opportunities to develop self-confidence, determination, and flexibility. They could not possibly have succeeded without these characteristics. This was especially true for the women who grew up in the first half of the century. (Marie Curie, perhaps the best known of all women scientists, faced similar problems in an earlier generation.) One older woman scientist says that successful women scientists in those days had to be "really tough cookies. . . . At one time it wasn't even acceptable to start [a career in science]. So if you started back then you were tough to begin with."

From adolescence on, these women had to fight prevailing opinion—starting with that of their parents. Their first task was to gain permission to seek a higher education. The parents of Lise Meitner, Rita Levi-Montalcini, Barbara McClintock, and Rosalind Franklin all objected strongly when their daughters proposed going to a university.

The parents' main concern was that a college education would make their daughters "unhappy." Levi-Montalcini's father reminded her of female relatives who had gone to college and, in his opinion, had been miserable all their lives as a result. McClintock's mother worried that Barbara would become "a strange person, a person that didn't belong to society . . . even . . . a college professor."

Unhappy was a polite word for *unmarriageable*. Few people of the time imagined that a woman could be happy without a husband and children, and few questioned the idea that a woman who became educated and pursued a scientific career would be extremely unlikely to marry. Indeed, most of the women scientists in this book born before 1930 did not marry. (Margaret Burbidge and R. Rajalakshmi are the exceptions.) They were anything but unhappy, however.

Many people in North America and Europe today expect young women to go to college. They no longer think that a woman's having a career makes her strange or prevents her from raising a family. But women scientists in many developing nations—and in some industrialized countries with strong traditional cultures, such as Japan—still face cultural expectations much like those that American and European women faced earlier in the century. Saeko Hayashi, the first woman to earn a Ph.D. in astronomy from Tokyo University, is only 36, but she has said, "People tried to discourage me from going . . . to any university. . . . They preferred that I stay home and be a good mother." Similarly, Lydia Makhubu says that in Africa, women are expected to quit school or work after their early twenties.

When poverty and lack of basic education are added to these cultural expectations, as they so often are in developing nations, the odds against a woman's becoming a scientist are almost astronomical. One correspondent who had worked in South America wrote to this author, "In the Third World countries where we served, girls were lucky to get through high school. Scientific careers would have been far beyond their reach."

Even after they overcame the opposition of their parents and obtained their degrees, women scientists had to continue fighting in order to advance in their careers. Lise Meitner had to work in a basement woodshop because the head of a German chemical institute would not allow women in the institute's regular laboratories. Margaret Burbidge was barred from using the telescopes at Mount Wilson Observatory because she was a woman. McClintock, Burbidge, and Rajalakshmi at times had trouble finding salaried faculty positions at least partly for the same reason.

Barriers today are more subtle, but they still exist. Women scientists find advancement ever harder as they move higher on university or company career ladders. In Japan, for example, 30.8 percent of the science students in universities are women, but only 2.6 percent of the full professors are. The situation is even worse in Africa, Lydia Makhubu reports. Even in the United States, only about 8 percent of science and engineering professors are women.

Advancement becomes especially difficult if a woman wants to have children. To gain either tenure (a permanent academic position) or an important position in industry, a woman has to work hardest during her thirties. These are the same years in which she is likely to be raising a family. Some women do manage to raise children while carrying on scientific careers, especially if their husbands help them. Of the women in this book, Margaret Burbidge, R. Rajalakshmi, Lydia Makhubu, and Biruté Galdikas did so. But many women may not be able to manage this juggling act. Faced with the incredible stresses of being "Supermom," they give up—and science is the loser.

Fighting family, cultural expectations, and institutional discrimination may have helped a few women develop the confidence, determination, and flexibility that served them well as scientists. But for every woman who succeeded in overcoming these obstacles, there surely were ten, or a hundred, or a thousand, who dropped out of science careers or were afraid even to start because of the formidable opposition they knew they would face. The loss to humanity of all these women's contributions is incalculable.

It is possible that such losses will be less in the future. In spite of the many problems that still exist, the situation for women scientists seems to be slowly improving. In the United States, the proportion of women among scientists and engineers earning doctoral degrees doubled between 1975 and 1991. The number of women scientists in business and industry quadrupled during the same period. More men are becoming willing to share housework and child care. Some companies are adopting more liberal policies about child care and parental leave, and some universities are considering more flexible paths to tenure.

Improvement is occurring in the rest of the world as well. R. Rajalakshmi says it is becoming "progressively easier" for young women to become scientists. Biruté Galdikas says that girls in Indonesia today do not face any greater obstacles to scientific careers than boys do. Women in Islamic countries are under especially strong pressure to stay at home, but Aslihan Yener points out that women in Turkey led archaeological expeditions even in her mother's time. In Saudi Arabia, women now outnumber men in some scientific and medical fields. Business and government leaders in Japan have concluded that they can prevent a future shortage of scientists and engineers only by attracting more women to science.

Growing numbers of women in science could bring important changes, not only in the conditions under which women scientists work, but also in science itself. "Of course men and women see things differently," says Geza Teleki, a primatologist (scientist who studies monkeys and apes). "There are things—gender, ethnicity, nationality—that we all come burdened with and these affect our science."

One example of these differences occurred in Teleki's own field, primatology. Earlier in the century, when most primatologists were men, scientists were sure that males dominated primate social groups. Observers of wild primates tended to focus on male activities, such as fighting. "The early studies mirrored our society's institutions, which were also based on male hierarchies," says Sarah Blaffer Hrdy, a well-known primatologist. When women such as Jane Goodall, Dian Fossey, and Biruté Galdikas began reporting their long-term observations of wild primates, however, they found that the females were often more important to the social groups than the males. "The females are there for the long term," says primatologist Linda Fedigan. "The males . . . stay with a group for maybe five years, then mov[e] on." Both the men and the women primatologists may have observed accurately, but each group discovered only part of the truth because it tended to focus on what it expected or wanted to see.

Scientists disagree about whether there is such a thing as a "feminine" or "masculine" way of doing science—or, if there is, whether it is determined by biology, culture, or some of both. Certainly there is no approach to science that all women or all men share. Some approaches, however, do seem to be more common among women than among men.

Women, for example, seem most interested in using science to solve practical problems, especially social problems. Men are more inclined to seek scientific knowledge for its own sake. For instance, R. Rajalakshmi studied biochemistry mostly so she could learn about the nutritional needs of mothers and children. Lydia Makhubu studied plant medicines used by African healers both to preserve the healers' knowledge and to make the medicines safer and more effective. Makhubu thinks women scientists can play an important role in helping developing areas such as Africa because of this practical focus. "Some of Africa's greatest concerns today include finding ways to increase food production, to manage natural resources and the environment, nutrition, improved health and education. These areas are . . . related to those in which women have traditionally found their functions."

A second possible difference between women and men in science is that women tend to emphasize cooperation, both in their own lives and in their views of nature, whereas men are more likely to stress competition. Relatedly, more women than men may be inclined to see nature in terms of whole systems made up of many interacting parts, rather than isolating "nature-in-pieces," to use Barbara McClintock's term. McClintock's devotion to her corn plants and "feeling for the organism" contrasted with most male geneticists' focus on the chemistry of individual genes. Biruté Galdikas emphasizes the connection between saving orangutans and preserving their rain forest home.

If increasing numbers of women do spread these views more widely in science, the change may benefit everyone. Focusing on interaction and cooperation seems more likely to solve today's complex social and environmental problems than the traditional "male" emphasis on separateness, competition, and science as a means of controlling nature.

It is important to remember, however, that none of these approaches is exclusively "feminine." Some men share them, and some women do not. Barbara McClintock's biographer, Evelyn Fox Keller, insists that McClintock "didn't adopt a masculine ideal, nor did she adopt a purely feminine ideal. She made use of the full range of human capacity . . . and all her intuitive strengths, in the service of science. . . . It doesn't matter that she was a woman. One could find men in that tradition as well."

Lise Meitner was the first to realize that the cores of atoms could be split, releasing tremendous energy. (Courtesy American Institute of Physics, Emilio Segre Visual Archives, Herzfeld Collection)

Lise Meitner

(1878–1968)

A flash of brilliant light, far brighter than the normal dawn, wiped out the desert sky. Seconds later, it was replaced by a rolling fireball of yellow and red. The fireball faded into a white cloud shaped like a mushroom, rising on a "stem" of smoke and dust. Within 20 seconds, the cloud towered more than a mile in the air.

The time was 5:30 A.M. on July 16, 1945. The United States had just tested its first atomic bomb. Using less than 20 pounds of material, the bomb's explosion had the same force as the blast from 20,000 tons of the conventional explosive TNT. Less than a month later, on August 8, an atomic bomb would be dropped on the city of Hiroshima in Japan. As a result, 130,000 people would be hurt or killed.

Neither mushroom clouds nor the deaths of thousands had been in the mind of Lise Meitner when she took a walk in the snow with her nephew in Sweden seven years before. A 60-year-old Jewish refugee from Nazi Germany, Meitner had simply wanted to explain the puzzling results of an experiment that a friend and fellow scientist, still in Germany, had just performed. But the insight she had that winter day was the root from which the terrible mushroom cloud—and the many useful things that came from atomic power—would grow.

Lise Meitner (LEE zuh MITE nur) was born on November 7, 1878, in Vienna, Austria. Philipp Meitner, her father, was a prosperous lawyer. Her mother, Hedwig, loved music. So did Lise, the third of the Meitners' eight children.

From childhood Lise displayed what she later called a "marked bent" for physics and mathematics. Her parents assumed that her education would stop after she attended a girls' high school, as most young women's did, but Lise had other ideas. She had read about Marie Curie, a Polish scientist who worked with her husband in France. In 1902, the Curies discovered a new chemical element called radium. Lise wanted to become a scientist like Marie Curie and explore radioactivity, the strange phenomenon displayed by elements like radium. They broke down naturally into other elements, meanwhile releasing energy.

At the age of 22, well after the age at which most women of her time had married, Lise Meitner told her parents that she wanted to enter the University of Vienna. The Meitners protested that few women gained admission to major universities. Fewer still could earn a living in science. When Lise insisted, however, they accepted her decision.

Meitner entered the university in 1901 and received her doctor's degree in 1905. She was only the 15th woman to earn a doctorate from the University of Vienna since its founding in 1365—and the first to receive one in physics.

In 1907, Meitner went to the University of Berlin, in Germany, to do advanced studies. A young chemist named Otto Hahn, already famous for work with radioactivity, agreed to take her on as his assistant. But Emil Fischer, the head of the university's chemical institute, refused to allow women in the institute's lecture rooms or laboratories. He insisted that Meitner work with Hahn only in a little basement room that had been designed as a woodshop. Even in those cramped quarters, Hahn's work with Meitner was happy and productive. On their best days, Meitner later recalled, "we sang together in two-part harmony, mostly songs by Brahms." Meitner's working conditions improved in 1912, when she and Hahn moved to the newly opened Kaiser Wilhelm Institutes in Dahlem, a suburb of Berlin.

World War I, which began in August 1914, interrupted their scientific activities. Hahn remained in the lab to do war-related research, while Meitner worked as a nurse and X-ray technician in a field hospital. Whenever she could get a break, she returned to continue her projects with Hahn.

Soon after the war ended in 1918, Hahn and Meitner announced that they had discovered a new element, the second-heaviest element known at that time. Like uranium and other heavy elements, it was radioactive. It slowly broke down to become a slightly lighter element called actinium. Meitner and Hahn called it proto-actinium, Latin for "before actinium." The name was later shortened to protactinium.

The discovery of protactinium made Meitner as well as Hahn famous. The Berlin Academy of Science awarded her the Leibniz Medal, and the Austrian Academy of Science gave her the Leiben Prize. In 1926 she became the first woman full physics professor in Germany, at the University of Berlin. By this time she was also head of a new department of radioactivity physics at the Kaiser Wilhelm Institutes. There she studied the kinds of energy, or rays, given off when radioactive elements broke down. She did not work with Hahn as often as before, but they remained close friends.

A militant political party called the National Socialists (Nazis) began to gain power in Germany during the 1920s. In 1933 they seized control of the German government.

The Nazis blamed Jews for all of Germany's problems. They passed laws that restricted Jewish people's activities and deprived them of property and civil rights. Although Meitner was of Jewish descent, she was safe from these laws at first because she was an Austrian citizen. Furthermore, as a famous scientist, she was (she wrote later) "too valuable to annoy." No one could say, though, how long her safety would last.

Meitner tried to ignore these alarming political events. She was much more interested in new discoveries that physicists were making about the structure of atoms. Since the turn of the century, scientists had known that atoms, once thought to be indivisible, were actually made up of smaller particles. Lightweight particles called electrons, which had a negative electric charge, circled a small, dense center, or nucleus. The nucleus contained heavier, positively charged particles called protons. Atoms of different elements had different numbers of protons. Then, in 1932, an English physicist named James Chadwick found a second kind of particle in the atomic nucleus. These particles had a neutral, or zero, electric charge. He called them neutrons.

Scientists found that they could use neutrons to learn more about atomic nuclei (plural of *nucleus*). Chadwick invented a "neutron gun" that gave off free neutrons, and a young Italian physicist named Enrico Fermi used it to bombard atoms. Fermi found that when an atomic nucleus captured a neutron, the nucleus gave off a beta ray. A beta ray is like an electron except that it comes from the nucleus. This loss in effect increases the charge of the nucleus by one, as if it had gained a proton. The atom therefore is changed into an atom of the next heavier element. Meitner and Hahn, among others, also tried bombarding heavy elements with neutrons.

On March 15, 1938, Germany seized control of Austria. All Austrian citizens automatically became citizens of Germany. This meant that Lise Meitner was now subject to Germany's anti-Jewish laws. Her job and even her life were in danger. She saw she would have to leave Germany at once.

Many Jews, including some of Germany's best scientists, had already fled the country. To stop this outflow, the German government refused to grant visas that would let Jews or scientists leave the country legally. With the help of

Hahn and other friends, however, Meitner obtained permission from the Dutch government to enter the Netherlands without a visa. She had to pretend she was merely taking a vacation, which meant she could bring just one small suitcase.

At the Dutch border, Meitner got what she later called "the scare of my life." A Nazi military patrol went through her train, checking everyone's passports. Meitner had only her Austrian passport, which had expired years ago. The patrol took the passport and disappeared for 10 minutes. Then they returned the passport and left without a word.

Meitner found a position at the Nobel Institute of Theoretical Physics in Stockholm, Sweden, and settled there. She tried to go on with her work, but she felt lonely and helpless. At the end of 1938, when Enrico Fermi and his wife, Laura, visited Meitner, Laura Fermi described Meitner as "a worried, tired woman with the tense expression that all refugees have in common."

Meitner was not completely friendless, however. Her nephew, Otto Frisch, had also become a physicist. He was then working in Denmark with Niels Bohr, who was famous for his work with atoms. Frisch and Meitner decided to celebrate the Christmas of 1938 together in Kungälv, a Swedish village.

While at Kungälv, Meitner received a startling letter from Otto Hahn. Hahn explained that he had been bombarding uranium with neutrons, much as Fermi had done. But

Lise Meitner, describing her feelings when a military patrol took her passport as she was fleeing Germany:

"I got so frightened, my heart almost stopped beating. I knew that the Nazis had just declared open season on Jews, that the hunt was on. For ten minutes I sat there and waited, minutes that seemed like so many hours."

instead of producing elements near uranium in atomic weight, he seemed somehow to have made a radioactive form of the element barium. Barium has 36 fewer protons than uranium. In order to make barium, Hahn's neutrons would have had to split the uranium nucleus almost in half. No theory had ever predicted that a neutron could split an atomic nucleus. Hahn asked Meitner if she had any idea what might have happened.

Meitner showed Hahn's letter to Otto Frisch, and the two took a walk in the snow to discuss it. Frisch wore skis, but Meitner, who enjoyed hiking, kept up with him on foot.

Hahn was too good a chemist to have simply made a mistake, Meitner insisted. But could he really have split an atom? Meitner and Frisch recalled Niels Bohr's latest view of the atomic nucleus, which pictured it as similar to a drop of liquid. A force called surface tension holds the molecules of a liquid drop together. Bohr believed that some force bound the particles in the nucleus together in a similar way.

But suppose, Meitner said, that the liquid drop—the nucleus—began to stretch until it was almost two drops, connected by a narrow "waist." Very little force would be needed to break the drop apart at the narrow spot. This was especially true because the electrical charge of a nucleus partly counteracted the force that held the nucleus together. Meitner and Frisch calculated that the electric charge of uranium was high enough to reduce the "surface tension" almost to zero. A uranium nucleus might thus be, as Frisch wrote later, "a very wobbly drop—like a large thin-walled balloon filled with water." It would be easy to split.

If Hahn had actually split uranium atoms, Meitner went on, energy should have been released. She and Frisch sat down on a fallen tree trunk and began making calculations on scraps of paper. Meitner found that the splitting should release an amazing 200 million electron volts per atom—20 million times more than an equivalent amount of TNT!

Such energy still would not have amounted to much in the tiny sample Hahn had been working with. He had not detected it because he was not looking for it. Frisch thought it should be easy to spot, however, with the right equipment.

Now as excited as his aunt, Frisch broke their visit short and returned to Denmark. He telephoned Meitner a few days later at her laboratory. When he had told Bohr about their ideas, Frisch reported, Bohr slapped his forehead and cried, "Oh, what idiots we all have been! This is just as it must be!" Bohr recalled that other scientists had also gotten some results from neutron bombardment that they could not explain. They must have been splitting atoms all along.

Frisch repeated Hahn's experiment, and his detectors found exactly the amount of energy that he and Meitner had predicted. The two began writing a paper about their discovery. Frisch suggested calling the splitting process *fission*, a term from biology that described how cells divided.

Soon physicists everywhere were talking about fission. Among them was Enrico Fermi, who was now living in the United States. Fermi realized something that even Meitner and Frisch had missed. When a neutron split a uranium atom, several more neutrons were released. These neutrons could hit other uranium nuclei, which would then split, release further neutrons, and so on. In other

Lise Meitner in a 1946 interview, speaking of possible peaceful uses of atomic energy:

"It's tempting to speculate . . . about uranium-charged trains and flivvers [cars], and—why not?—about a trip to the moon . . . in rockets propelled by atomic energy. But . . . neither our generation nor the next one will sample the possibilities of atomic energy."

words, if the amount of uranium was large enough, a chain reaction would be created. Just a few split atoms would quickly become billions, releasing tremendous energy. An uncontrolled chain reaction could be used to make a bomb that would destroy a whole city.

On September 1, 1939, just a few months after Meitner and Frisch's fission paper was published, World War II began. Sweden remained neutral during the war, so Meitner was safe. But she was unhappy because, with Hahn still in Germany and Fermi and several others in the United States, she had friends on both sides of the conflict.

Germany surrendered on May 7, 1945, but the war between the United States and Germany's ally, Japan, continued. Then, on August 6, the United States dropped an atomic bomb on the Japanese city of Hiroshima. To Meitner the news was "a terrible surprise, like a bolt of lightning out of the blue." It was the first she knew of the secret race of Fermi and other scientists in the United States to develop such a bomb before Germany did. Three days later, another bomb was dropped on a second Japanese city, Nagasaki. Japan surrendered on August 14, ending the war.

Meitner suddenly found herself famous as the woman whose flash of inspiration had led to the atomic bomb. In the many interviews she gave after the war, she emphasized that she had never worked directly on the bomb. She said, "It is an unfortunate accident that this discovery came about in time of war. . . . You must not blame us scientists for the use to which war technicians have put our discoveries."

Otto Hahn won a Nobel Prize in physics for his part in the discovery of nuclear fission. For unknown reasons, Meitner was not so honored. She did, however, receive many other awards, such as the Max Planck Medal, which Germany gave her in 1949. In 1966 she also received the Enrico Fermi Award, a $50,000 prize given yearly by the U.S. Atomic Energy Commission to scientists making important discov-

Meitner's insight indirectly led to the atomic bomb, but news of the bomb dropped on Hiroshima, Japan, struck her "like a bolt of lightning out of the blue." The bomb, dropped on August 6, 1945, was carried by a plane whose wing can be seen in the corner of this picture.
(Courtesy Library of Congress)

eries in atomic research. Otto Hahn and Fritz Strassmann, Hahn's assistant at the time of his fission experiment, were given the award as well. The three were the first foreign scientists to receive the prize. Meitner was the first woman.

Lise Meitner continued to live and do research in Sweden for many years, although she officially retired in 1947. She stopped work in 1960 and moved to England to live near Otto Frisch, who by then was a professor at Cambridge University. Even after that, she often gave lectures abroad and took long hikes in the Austrian mountains. She died on October 27, 1968.

In an autobiographical article called "Looking Back," Meitner wrote that she had decided at an early age that her life "need not be easy provided only it was not empty." She certainly got her wish. Many parts of her life were not easy, but it was a life very full of friendship, scientific adventure, and achievement.

Beginning in 1940, scientists learned how to make artificial elements heavier than uranium. In 1982, German physicists created a new element later named meitnerium in honor of Lise Meitner. The team's leader called Meitner "the most significant woman scientist of this century."

Chronology

November 7, 1878	Lise Meitner born in Vienna, Austria
1901	enters University of Vienna
1905	receives doctor's degree in physics
1907	begins work with Otto Hahn in Berlin
1912	moves to Kaiser Wilhelm Institutes
1914	World War I begins
1918	World War I ends; Meitner and Hahn announce discovery of protactinium
1926	Meitner becomes Germany's first woman full physics professor
1933	Nazis take control of German government
1938	Germany takes control of Austria; Meitner flees to Sweden
December 1938	Meitner and Otto Frisch realize that Otto Hahn has split atomic nucleus
1939	Meitner and Frisch publish paper on nuclear fission; World War II begins
August 1945	U.S. drops atomic bombs on Hiroshima and Nagazaki; World War II ends

1947	Meitner officially retires but continues research in Sweden
1960	Meitner stops work and moves to England
1966	receives Enrico Fermi Award
October 27, 1968	Meitner dies

Further Reading

Axelson, George. "Is the Atom Terror Exaggerated?" *Saturday Evening Post*, January 5, 1946. Excellent interview with Meitner, reviewing her life and considering the future of atomic energy.

Crawford, Deborah. *Lise Meitner, Atomic Pioneer*. New York: Crown, 1969. For young adults. May be only book-length biography of Meitner. Some fictionalized dialogue but mostly factual; provides good scientific background.

Hahn, Otto. *Otto Hahn: A Scientific Autobiography*, translated and edited by Willy Ley. New York: Scribners, 1966. Includes many descriptions of Hahn's work with Meitner.

Hermann, Armin. *The New Physics: The Route into the Atomic Age*. Bonn-Bad Godesberg: Inter Nationes, 1979. Includes interesting quotations, details, and documents pertaining to atomic physics in first half of the 20th century; puts Meitner's work in scientific context.

Lightman, Alan P. "To Cleave an Atom." *Science 84*, November 1984. Describes Christmas meeting at which Meitner and Frisch worked out details of nuclear fission and places it in context of other discoveries about atoms.

McGrayne, Sharon. *Nobel Prize Women in Science*. New York: Carol Communications/Birch Lane Press, 1993. For young adults. Includes excellent chapter on Meitner.

Meitner, Lise. "Looking Back." *Bulletin of the Atomic Scientists*, November 1964. Meitner recalls her life.

"Meitner, Lise." *Current Biography*, 1945. Good, brief description of Meitner's career up to that time.

Barbara McClintock brought new understanding of how the genetic information passed on from parents to offspring can change living things. (Courtesy Cold Spring Harbor Laboratory Archives)

Barbara McClintock

(1902–1992)

An environment can change over time. Imagine a plain that was once green and full of life. But the climate changed, and now the land is slowly becoming a desert. Plants and animals are struggling to adapt to a new life without water. Only a few kinds will survive.

According to Charles Darwin's theory of evolution, the survivors will be those who happen to be born a little different from their parents. Perhaps their bodies can store water better or make do with a little less. Information "coded" into these creatures' cells can pass on these characteristics, or traits, to their offspring. Darwin's theory said that the survivors of a changed environment owed their lives strictly to chance. But today, many scientists think this that is not entirely true. Hereditary, or genetic, information may be able to respond to harsh conditions by increasing the chance that changes in traits will occur. This increase improves the odds for survival.

This new view of evolution has arisen from partly the work of Barbara McClintock, who spent what might seem to be a lonely life studying corn plants. Her discoveries shed light on how living things develop before birth and respond to challenges in their environment.

Barbara McClintock preferred being alone almost from the time of her birth in Hartford, Connecticut, on June 16, 1902. McClintock later recalled, "my mother used to put a pillow on the floor, and give me one toy and just leave me there. She said I didn't cry, didn't call for anything."

Barbara's father, Thomas Henry McClintock, was a company doctor for Standard Oil Corporation. After 1908, he and his family lived in Brooklyn, then on the edge of New York City. He took care of the crews of the Standard tankers that docked at the busy Brooklyn shipyard. His wife, Sara Handy McClintock, had her hands full taking care of four children, of whom Barbara was the third.

The McClintocks encouraged their children to be independent. They did not even make the youngsters go to school. (Laws did not require school attendance at that time.) When the children did go, the McClintocks insisted that they not be given homework. Even so, Barbara grew up with a love of reading and study. She loved to sit by herself, "thinking about things." While at Erasmus Hall High School, she began to turn her thinking toward science.

Independence was all very well, but Barbara's mother thought that wanting to go to college was taking it too far. She worried that if Barbara became too well educated, no young man would want to marry her. She also pointed out that, with Thomas McClintock serving overseas as a military surgeon in World War I, the family had no money for college tuition.

Barbara McClintock, explaining why her mother did not want her to go to college:

"[She feared that I would become] a strange person, a person that didn't belong to society. . . . She was even afraid I might become a college professor."

But Barbara, like Lise Meitner, insisted, and when her father came home, he agreed with her. She entered the College of Agriculture at Cornell University in Ithaca, New York, in 1919. She probably chose this school both because the tuition was free and because Cornell was one of the few coeducational universities that encouraged women to study science.

Barbara McClintock was so popular during her first year at college that she was elected president of the women's freshman class. After her first two years, however, she gave up most of her nonacademic interests, including dating. One exception was music. Even in her senior year, she played tenor banjo in a jazz improvisation group.

In her later undergraduate years, McClintock devoted her attention to science. Yet at first, she said, "there was absolutely no thought of a career. I was just having a marvelous time." In her junior year she took her first courses in genetics, the study of how living things inherit traits from their parents. By the time she graduated in 1923, she had decided to stay in that field.

Unfortunately, Cornell's plant breeding department, in which genetics was taught, did not accept women graduate students. McClintock therefore joined the botany (plant science) department instead. There she began studying inheritance in maize, or Indian corn. The kernels (seeds) on ears of this corn have different colors, and the patterns of color are inherited. At the time, most research on genetics was done on maize or fruit flies.

McClintock made her first major discovery while she was still a graduate student. Scientists knew that hereditary information was carried on chromosomes, pairs of ribbonlike structures in each cell. One chromosome carried many pieces of information. Each chromosome pair was different from the others, although both members of a pair were alike. Geneticists had learned to identify particular chromosomes

McClintock used maize, or Indian corn, in her genetic experiments because the different colors of its kernels are determined by heredity. (Courtesy Lisa Yount)

in fruit flies by noting differences in the chromosomes' shape and color, but no one had been able to do this with maize. McClintock, however, quickly worked out a way to tell the 10 pairs of maize chromosomes apart.

McClintock received her master's degree in botany in 1925 and her Ph.D. in 1927. Cornell then hired her as an instructor. During the next several years she did pioneering research that showed how changes in whole maize plants were related to changes in the plant cells' chromosomes. Her most important experiment on this subject, done in 1931 with an assistant named Harriet Creighton, has been called "one of the truly great experiments of modern biology."

This experiment gave McClintock a national reputation in genetics, but it did not get her a decent job. Cornell, like most coeducational universities of the time, seldom promoted women beyond the lowest ranks of its faculty. McClintock refused to accept such discrimination. She left Cornell in 1931, soon after her landmark research was published.

During the early 1930s McClintock led an academic gypsy life. She lived on grants and drove back and forth across the country in an old Model A Ford, dividing her time among three universities. She enjoyed her travels, but she wanted a permanent job. Faculty positions were as hard to find as other jobs during that era of economic depression, but men as well qualified as she was had little trouble obtaining them. McClintock resented the fact that she could not.

The University of Missouri at Columbia, one of the three schools at which she had done part-time research, finally hired McClintock as an assistant professor in 1936. While there, she did experiments to find out how X rays damaged chromosomes and produced mutations, or changes in genetic information.

McClintock and the university were not happy with each other. The university administration found McClintock's behavior too unconventional. When she accidentally locked herself out of her laboratory one weekend, for example, she simply climbed up the side of the building and went in through a window. McClintock, in turn, resented the fact that, although her reputation in genetics continued to grow—she was elected vice president of the Genetics Society of America in 1939, for example—she was never promoted or even invited to faculty meetings. She finally quit in 1941.

Fortunately, an old friend told McClintock about the genetics research laboratory at Cold Spring Harbor, New York. The laboratory was managed by the Carnegie Institution of Washington, which steel magnate and philanthropist Andrew Carnegie had founded. McClintock visited Cold Spring Harbor and liked it. Another old friend became its director shortly afterward, and he offered McClintock a permanent position there in 1942. Cold Spring Harbor gave McClintock security and a place to do her work without interference. She remained there for the rest of her life.

In 1944, scientists discovered that hereditary information is carried in the complex molecules of a chemical called DNA, short for deoxyribonucleic acid. DNA is contained in the chromosomes. Every DNA molecule holds thousands of genes, or units of hereditary information. Each gene determines one trait.

This discovery changed the focus of genetics. Instead of studying whole organisms such as fruit flies or maize plants, or even whole cells, most geneticists turned to DNA and other chemicals found inside cells. When they did study living things, they studied very simple ones, such as bacteria. But Barbara McClintock stayed with her maize.

In the 1940s, McClintock's maize began giving her ideas as revolutionary as Lise Meitner's proposal that the nucleus of an atom could be split. Like Meitner, McClintock refused to doubt her insight, even though it did not agree with accepted theories. "You let the material tell you where to go," she always said.

First, McClintock found a spot on the short arm of maize chromosome 9 at which the chromosome was unusually likely to break. She called this gene or group of genes at this spot Ds, for "dissociator," because it seemed to cause breakage. Cells in which Ds was active were very likely to contain mutations.

But Ds, McClintock discovered, caused chromosome breakage only when another gene was also present. She called this gene Ac, for "activator." Ac was on the long arm of chromosome 9, some distance away from Ds. Ac could be identified only by the effect it produced on Ds.

After more experiments, McClintock concluded that Ac was really a group of identical genes. When a cell divides, the chromosomes copy themselves so that each of the two "daughter" cells gets a complete set. McClintock found that during this process, one or more Ac genes sometimes was taken from one daughter cell and added to the other. The more copies of Ac a cell received, the higher the cell's mutation rate became.

McClintock's work showed, for the first time, that there were two kinds of genes. Functional, or structural, genes control traits such as leaf or kernel color. Controlling genes, which had not been recognized before, affect whether and how structural genes will operate. Both Ds and Ac were controlling genes.

Later experiments showed McClintock that Ac could make Ds break free from its usual spot on the chromosome and move to another place. If Ds landed next to a structural gene, it made that gene inactive. If Ac made Ds move again, the structural gene became active once more. Ac could also move itself, sometimes even to another chromosome.

McClintock called the phenomenon of moving genes *transposition*. She concluded that it was a controlled, system-

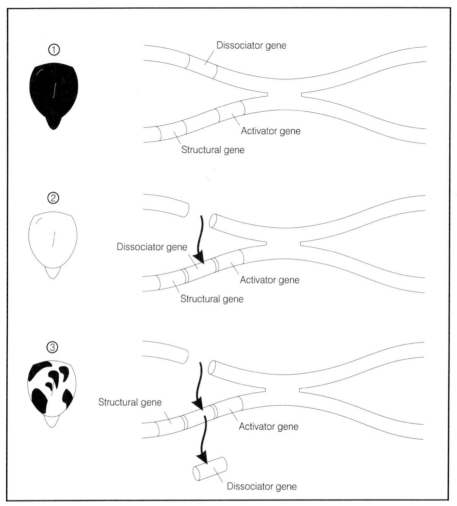

1. A structural gene coding for dark color makes a maize kernel dark. 2. If an activator gene makes a dissociator gene "jump" next to the structural gene, the structural gene no longer functions. As a result, the kernel is white. 3. If the activator gene makes the dissociator gene move again in some cells of the kernel, the structural gene becomes active again in those cells. The result is a kernel with dark spots (where the structural gene is active) and light spots (where it is not). (Courtesy Katherine MacFarlane)

atic process, not random as mutations were. Genes such as *Ac* somehow controlled their own activity as well as that of other genes. She thought transposition might be part of the process by which an organism develops before birth. It could help to turn genes on and off as the fertilized egg divides into many cells that mature into different types.

Transposition might also help an organism respond to stress, McClintock believed. When a living thing faced a major change in its environment, gene combinations like *Ac* and *Ds* might speed up its cells' rate of mutation. This would help the organism change its genome, or collection of genes. The more changes occurred, the greater the chance that some would help the organism adapt to its changed environment. In effect, controlling genes could speed up evolution.

McClintock gave a talk about her discoveries at Cold Spring Harbor in 1951. She was met with blank stares and even some laughter. She got a similar response when she tried again to present her ideas in the mid-1950s.

This chilly reaction "really knocked" McClintock, she recalled later. She knew she had presented plenty of evidence to prove her points. What could have gone wrong?

Part of the answer seems to have been that McClintock provided almost too much evidence. Geneticists though they were, most of McClintock's audience were not as familiar with maize genetics as she was. They therefore found her presentations hard to follow. But a more important problem was that she was proposing ideas that were completely opposed to the beliefs of most scientists at the time. Geneticists usually pictured genes as beads on a string. They believed that, except through random mutations, genes could not change—let alone move. Above all, genes could not actively respond to their environment. Such an idea seemed to go against the theory of evolution, which held that all adaptation arose out of chance mutations.

McClintock did not let this rejection stop her work. "If you know you're right, you don't care. You know that sooner or later, it will all come out in the wash," she said later. She did, however, stop trying to explain her ideas. She published accounts of her experiments only in the Carnegie Institution's yearbooks. In turn, most other scientists forgot about her. One referred to her as "just an old bag who'd been hanging around Cold Spring Harbor for years."

Nonetheless, recognition of McClintock's work slowly began to mount in the late 1960s. She received the Kimber Genetics Award from the National Academy of Sciences in 1967, the same year in which she officially retired. (In fact her research schedule continued unchanged.) In 1970 she was awarded the National Medal of Science.

Only in the late 1970s, however, did other scientists' work begin to support McClintock's in a major way. Some found viruses that could carry genes from one bacterium to another. The viruses inserted the genes in the bacteria's chromosomes, where the genes functioned normally. Other scientists found transposable elements, or "jumping genes" as they began to be called, in fruit flies and other higher organisms, including humans. They discovered several systems of controlling genes.

This new recognition brought McClintock a flood of honors in the late 1970s. In 1978 she won the Louis S. Rosenstiel Award and the Louis and Bert Freedman Foundation Award. McClintock won eight awards in 1981. The three most important—the MacArthur Laureate Award, the Lasker Award, and Israel's Wolf Prize—came in a single week. McClintock regretted the publicity that the honors brought. In one interview she complained, "It's too much. . . . At my age I should be allowed to do as I please and have my fun." "Fun" to McClintock was undisturbed work in laboratory and cornfield.

But the biggest award and greatest publicity of all were still to come. On October 10, 1983, McClintock learned that she had won the Nobel Prize in physiology or medicine. She was the first woman to win a physiology or medicine prize that was unshared with other scientists. One of her few comments about the prize was, "It seems a little unfair to reward a person for having so much pleasure over the years."

McClintock received her prize in Stockholm on December 10, 1983, when she was 81 years old. The Nobel committee called her work "one of the two great discoveries of our times in genetics." (The other was the discovery in 1953 of the structure of the DNA molecule.) The audience at Nobel ceremonies is normally quiet, but McClintock received so much applause that the floor shook.

McClintock's life changed little after her Nobel award. She quietly continued her research almost until her death. She died on September 2, 1992, just a few months after her 90th birthday.

In honoring Barbara McClintock, the scientific world recognized more than a series of important discoveries and a lifetime of dedicated work. It also paid delayed respect to a way of studying living things that was very different from the one that still dominates most laboratories. Most geneticists focus on the chemical effects of individual genes. McClintock, by contrast, had what science historian Evelyn Fox Keller calls "a feeling for the organism"—the living thing as a whole. McClintock always saw genes in terms of the way they affected real, living corn plants.

Chromosomes and genes, in turn, became almost like living things to McClintock. "The more I worked with them the bigger and bigger [they] got," she once said. "I wasn't outside, I was down there [in the

I start with the |corn| seedling, and I don't want to leave it. I don't feel I really know the story if I don't watch the plant all the way along. So I know every plant in the field. I know them intimately, and I find it a great pleasure to know them.

—Barbara McClinock

cell]. I was part of the system . . . and these [chromosomes] were my friends. "

Many people saw Barbara McClintock's life as lonely and perhaps unhappy, but she herself never found it so. She had human friends, and she had "friends" among the corn stalks and the chromosomes. Above all, she had the joy that her work brought her. Near the end of her life she told an interviewer, "I've had such a good time. . . . I've had a very, very satisfying and interesting life. "

Chronology

June 16, 1902	Barbara McClintock born in Hartford, Connecticut
1919	enters Cornell University
1923	graduates from Cornell
1925	receives master's degree in botany
1927	receives Ph.D. degree
1931	shows how changes in plants are related to changes in chromosomes; leaves Cornell
early 1930s	does short research projects at several universities
1936	hired by University of Missouri; does work on mutations caused by X rays
1941	leaves University of Missouri
1942	joins Cold Spring Harbor Laboratory
1940s	discovers genes that control other genes
early 1950s	presents reports about moving and controlling genes and is rejected; continues research
1967	receives Kimber Genetics Award; officially retires but continues work

1970	receives National Medal of Science
late 1970s	other scientists' work confirms McClintock's
1981	McClintock wins eight awards
December 10, 1983	wins Nobel Prize in physiology or medicine
September 2, 1992	McClintock dies

Further Reading

Dash, Joan. *The Triumph of Discovery*. New York: Julian Messner, 1991. For young adults. Includes good chapter on McClintock.

Federoff, Nina, and David Botstein, eds. *The Dynamic Genome*. New York: Cold Spring Harbor Laboratory Press, 1992. Includes reminiscences by people who knew McClintock and reprints of some of her most important papers. Parts are difficult reading.

Keller, Evelyn Fox. *A Feeling for the Organism*. San Francisco: W. H. Freeman, 1983. Full-length adult biography of McClintock, based on interviews with her.

———. "McClintock's Maize." *Science 81*, October 1981. Concise review of McClintock's life and most important ideas.

Kittredge, Mary. *Barbara McClintock*. New York: Chelsea House, 1991. Book-length biography of McClintock for young adults.

Lewin, Roger. "A Naturalist of the Genome." *Science*, October 28, 1983. Review of McClintock's ideas written just after she won the Nobel Prize.

"McClintock, Barbara." *Current Biography*, 1984. Concise account of McClintock's life.

McGrayne, Sharon. *Nobel Prize Women in Science*. New York: Carol Communications/Birch Lane Press, 1993. For young adults. Contains excellent chapter on McClintock.

Wallis, Claudia. "Honoring a Modern Mendel." *Time*, October 24, 1983. Brief, clear explanation of McClintock's ideas, written just after she won the Nobel Prize.

Rita Levi-Montalcini discovered nerve growth factor (NGF), a natural sub-stance that makes nerves grow. (Courtesy Washington University, St. Louis)

Rita Levi-Montalcini

(1909–)

Several years ago, Naomi began to become forgetful. Now she can no longer recognize her family. She cannot feed or dress herself. She suffers from Alzheimer's disease, a breakdown of the brain that strikes some older people.

Pablo has been in a wheelchair since a motorcycle accident damaged his spine. Determinedly he has continued his studies in law school. Never again, though, can he run with his friends on the college track team.

Doctors today can do little to help Naomi regain her mental powers or Pablo walk again. Someday, however, they may have treatments that will let people like these replace damaged nerve cells. Such treatments could grow out of the work of an Italian scientist named Rita Levi-Montalcini.

Doing some of her early studies in a makeshift laboratory in her bedroom, Levi-Montalcini discovered a substance that makes nerves grow. This chemical, called nerve growth factor (NGF), helps the nervous system develop before birth. Someday it may be used as a medical treatment as well.

Rita Levi-Montalcini was born on April 22, 1909, in Turin, Italy. Her father, Adamo Levi, was an engineer and factory owner. Rita admired his energy and intelligence, but his fierce temper and stern ways made her a little afraid of him. She felt closer to her gentle mother, Adele Montalcini (mont ahl CHEE nee) Levi, whose maiden name Rita later used as part of her professional name.

Rita's best friend was her twin sister, Paola. She also admired Gino and Anna, her older brother and sister. The four grew up in a large, comfortable house in Turin, an industrial city in northern Italy. Like Lise Meitner's family, the Levis were Jewish, but Adamo Levi did not have strong ties to any religion. He told his children that, if asked about their religion, they should answer, "We are freethinkers."

When Rita was 20, she watched a beloved family friend die of cancer. This made her decide to go to medical school. Her mother supported her decision, but her father had doubts. Like Lise Meitner's parents and Barbara McClintock's mother, he felt that higher education was "unsuitable for a woman" and would make Rita unhappy. Still, he did not forbid her to try it.

Rita Levi-Montalcini enrolled in the Turin School of Medicine in the fall of 1930. She graduated as an M.D. six years later. Her favorite class in medical school was anatomy, the structure of the body. When she looked at body tissues through the microscope, she became fascinated by the spider-like cells of the nervous system. The anatomy professor, Giuseppe Levi, was not a relative, but his energy and fierce temper made Rita think of her father. She and Levi remained friends all their lives.

While Levi-Montalcini was still a teenager, Benito Mussolini had made himself dictator of Italy. Mussolini's Fascist party shared many beliefs with the Nazis in Germany, who were rising to power at about the same time. Mussolini's government, following the lead of the Nazis, began a campaign of persecution against Jews in 1936. The persecution was not as severe as in Germany. Still, in 1938, the same year Lise Meitner fled Germany, the Italian government passed a law that suspended all Jews from jobs in universities. This meant that Levi-Montalcini lost the position as Giuseppe Levi's assistant that she had held since her graduation two years earlier.

Conditions became still harder when World War II began and Italy joined the war on the German side. Unable to find work, Levi-Montalcini confided her frustrations to a friend from medical school. He suggested that she set up a small laboratory at home and continue the research on the nervous systems of unborn (embryo) chickens that she had been doing at the medical school. "One doesn't lose heart in the face of the first difficulties," he insisted.

Levi-Montalcini realized that some parts of her work could be done at home, since chicken eggs with embryos were easy to obtain and keep alive. Carrying out her research in spite of the anti-Jewish laws seemed like "a voyage of adventure to unknown lands." The idea thrilled her.

With the help of her family, Levi-Montalcini set up a "private laboratory *a la* Robinson Crusoe" in her bedroom. A small, thermostat-controlled heater became the incubator in which she kept her eggs. She sharpened sewing needles to make tiny scalpels for cutting apart the embryos. The only expensive items she used were two microscopes.

Levi-Montalcini's main project was repeating some experiments done by a scientist named Viktor Hamburger. Normally, as a chick embryo's limbs develop, cells grow out from the spinal cord and enter the limbs. The cells mature and become the nerves of the limbs. Hamburger had shown that, if a developing limb was cut off, the spinal cord cells that would have grown into it failed to complete their development. Hamburger thought the limb produced some substance that made the spinal cord cells mature.

Levi-Montalcini's experiments showed that the spinal cord cells did become mature nerve cells. When they reached the stump of the cut limb, however, they died. She suspected that the substance made by the limb kept the young cells healthy and made them grow toward the limb, rather than helping them mature.

Unlike the Nazis, the Fascists seldom physically attacked Jewish citizens. The greatest danger Levi-Montalcini and her family faced during the first part of the war was from bombs dropped on Turin by the Allies (countries that opposed Germany and Italy). To escape the bombs, the Levis moved to a small house in the nearby hills. Levi-Montalcini's laboratory then became just a corner of a large room that the whole family shared. When she was through with her eggs, they went into the family's meals.

Mussolini resigned control of the Italian government on July 25, 1943. German troops took over the country a month and a half later. Now the Levis and other Italian Jews faced the same kind of danger Lise Meitner had faced when the Germans took over Austria. Along with thousands of other refugees, the Levis fled south. They hoped to find safety with Allied troops, who were moving north along the Italian peninsula.

The Levis ended up in Florence, where a friend of Paola's helped them

Rita Levi-Montalcini, explaining how she could concentrate on research during a war that threatened her freedom and possibly her life:

"The answer lies in the desperate . . . desire of human beings to ignore what is happening in situations where full awareness might lead one to self-destruction."

find a room in a boarding house. They lived there for about a year. Like other Jewish refugees, they carried false identity cards with non-Jewish names. Rita and Paola made fake identity cards for other refugees.

The Allies freed Italy from German control in the spring of 1945, and the Levis returned to Turin soon afterward. At first, Levi-Montalcini went back to her old job as Giuseppe Levi's assistant. In the summer of 1946, however, she received a letter from Viktor Hamburger. He had read a paper about her experiments that had been published during the war. He was at Washington University in St. Louis, Missouri, and he invited Levi-Montalcini to come there for a semester and do further research with him. That "one-semester" visit lasted 30 years.

Levi-Montalcini went to the United States in September 1946. For several years she continued to study how nerve cells grew, moved, and died as chick embryos developed. Then, early in 1950, Hamburger mentioned that a former student of his, Elmer Bueker, had recently grafted tissue from a mouse cancer onto a chick embryo. The cancer tissue caused nerve cells from ganglia (bundles of nerve fibers) in the embryo to multiply and send fibers into the tumor. An extra limb grafted onto the embryo would have had the same effect. But why should a cancer make nerve cells grow?

Levi-Montalcini repeated Bueker's experiments. She found a kind of mouse tumor (cancer) that made chick embryo nerve fibers grow into the tumor, just as Bueker had said. But she noticed that, unlike the fibers that would have been stimulated by a grafted limb, these fibers did not connect to cells in the cancer tissue. Levi-Montalcini suspected that the tumor tissue's effect was different from that of an extra limb.

She became positive of this when she looked at the effects of a second kind of mouse tumor in the fall of 1950. What she saw under her microscope "was so extraordinary that I thought I might be hallucinating." Not only the tumor but also the normal organs in the part of the embryo nearest the tumor were invaded by a thick network of nerve fibers. Nerves usually would not have arrived at these organs at that stage of development.

Nerve fibers had even grown into the embryo's veins, where they would never normally go. They had not grown into the arteries, however. Levi-Montalcini knew that the veins, but not the arteries, would carry waste products from the tumor into the embryo. She concluded that the tumor must put out some liquid that both speeded and attracted the growth of nerve cells. Its effect was much more powerful than that of substances produced by a limb.

To learn more about the "nerve-growth promoting agent," Levi-Montalcini decided to study it in tissue culture. In tissue culture, masses of cells are grown in laboratory dishes or test tubes. She knew that Hertha Meyer, another pupil of Giuseppe Levi, headed a tissue culture laboratory in Rio de Janeiro, Brazil. Levi-Montalcini obtained permission to work in Meyer's laboratory for a few months.

Levi-Montalcini landed in Rio in September 1952. Peering through holes in a small box in her overcoat pocket were two white mice, bearing the tumors she would need for her work.

At first Levi-Montalcini's research seemed to be failing. When she cultured bits of mouse tumor tissue together with chick embryo ganglia, the tumor did not make nerve fibers grow as she had hoped. But back in St. Louis, she had noticed that tumors that had been transplanted from one embryo to another produced more nerve growth than tumors that had been grown on an embryo only once. She decided to test tumors that had already grown in embryos.

The experiment was more successful than Levi-Montalcini had dared to dream. This time nerve fibers grew in a dense halo all around the ganglia, "radiating out like rays from the sun." No such effect appeared when she grew the

When Levi-Montalcini treated groups of nerve cells with a substance from mouse cancers, the substance made nerve fibers grow from the cells "like rays from the sun." (Courtesy Katherine MacFarlane)

ganglia alone or with other normal or cancerous tissues. By Christmastime, Levi-Montalcini had convinced herself that the tumors' effect in tissue culture was caused by the same substance as the tumors' effect on whole embryos. "The tumor effect exists!" she wrote excitedly to Hamburger.

When Levi-Montalcini returned to St. Louis in January 1953, Viktor Hamburger introduced her to a young scientist named Stanley Cohen. Cohen was an expert in biochemistry, the chemistry of living things. He would try to learn the chemical nature of the nerve-stimulating substance, which the group soon began calling nerve growth factor, or NGF. Levi-Montalcini, meanwhile, would study NGF's effects on embryos.

Like Otto Hahn and Lise Meitner, Levi-Montalcini and Cohen worked together splendidly from the start. "You and I [alone] are good," Cohen told Levi-Montalcini one day, "but together we are wonderful." The next six years, which Levi-Montalcini later called the "most intense and productive years of my life," proved him right.

Cohen's tests showed that NGF was a protein, one of a large class of chemicals commonly found in living things. He and Levi-Montalcini found that it did not have to come from cancer tissue. Some normal tissues produced it as well. Scientists can now also make NGF artificially.

Cohen and Levi-Montalcini's research partnership ended early in 1959. Levi-Montalcini had been made a full professor at the university in 1958, but Hamburger found he could not afford to offer Cohen a permanent position. To Levi-Montalcini this news was "like the tolling of a funeral bell." Cohen felt he needed more security, and he reluctantly left Washington University.

Levi-Montalcini had become a U.S. citizen in 1956, but she had also kept her Italian citizenship. She had stayed in touch with her family by means of long letters and yearly visits. Now she found that she wanted to be closer to her aging mother (her father had died before the war) and her twin, Paola, who had become a well-known artist.

To enable herself to spend more time in Italy, Levi-Montalcini arranged to set up a small research unit in Rome that would be connected to Washington University. She began spending three months in Italy each year, then six. In 1977 she decided to remain there permanently. She now lives in an apartment in Rome with Paola.

In 1969 Levi-Montalcini's research unit was greatly enlarged. It became part of the Laboratory of Cell Biology, run by Italy's National Council of Research. Levi-Montalcini was director of the laboratory from 1969 to 1979.

> For a long time [in the late 1960s and early 1970s] people didn't mention how NGF was discovered. . . . People repeated my experiment and didn't mention my name! I am not a person to be bitter, but it was astonishing to find it completely canceled.
>
> —Rita Levi-Montalcini

Levi-Montalcini retired in 1979 but, like Lise Meitner and Barbara McClintock, continued to do research. "The moment you stop working, you are dead," she told an interviewer. In 1986 she found that NGF affects cells in the brain as well as in the spinal cord and other nerves. This means that NGF might be able to make new brain cells grow to replace those damaged by accident or illness.

Even more surprising, Levi-Montalcini discovered that NGF affects certain cells in the immune system, which helps the body resist disease. Some immune cells even make NGF. Recent discoveries by other scientists have also linked the immune system and the nervous system. Such findings suggest that mental health and physical health are closely related.

Other scientists have found that living things produce several growth factors besides NGF. Stanley Cohen discovered one that makes skin cells grow, for example. Overproduction of these growth factors may play a role in some cancers. Lack of them may cause other health problems.

As interest in NGF grew and other growth factors were discovered, Levi-Montalcini received more and more awards for her work. In 1968 she was elected to the prestigious U.S. National Academy of Sciences; she was only the 10th woman to be chosen as a member. In September 1986, like Barbara McClintock, she won an Albert Lasker Memorial Research Award. A month later, also as with McClintock, Levi-Montalcini learned that she had won the Nobel Prize in physiology or medicine. She shared the prize with Stanley Cohen.

Interestingly, Levi-Montalcini's autobiography speaks of the Nobel Prize as being given, not to her, but to NGF itself. She pictures "him" as a mysterious human figure.

Wrapped in a black mantle, he bowed before the king [of Sweden, who presented the prizes] and, for a moment, lowered the veil covering his face. We recognized each other in a matter of seconds when I saw him looking for me among the applauding crowd. He then replaced his veil and disappeared as suddenly as he had appeared.

Someday, people may owe their recovered health to Levi-Montalcini's lifelong pursuit of this "mystery man."

Chronology

April 22, 1909	Rita Levi-Montalcini born in Turin, Italy
1930	enters Turin School of Medicine
1936	graduates with M.D. degree; Fascist persecution of Jews begins
1938	anti-Jewish laws deprive Levi-Montalcini of medical school job
1939–43	Levi-Montalcini does chick embryo research in bedroom during World War II
1943	Germany takes control of Italy; Levis live in hiding in Florence
1945	Allies free Italy; Levis return to Turin
1946	Levi-Montalcini goes to United States to do research with Viktor Hamburger
1950	discovers that some cancer tumors produce substance that makes nerve cells grow
1952	tissue culture research in Brazil proves that nerve-stimulating substance exists
1953–58	research with Stanley Cohen shows nature of nerve growth factor
1959	sets up small research unit in Italy
1968	elected to National Academy of Sciences

| 1969–79 | directs Laboratory of Cell Biology in Rome |
| 1986 | wins Lasker Award and Nobel Prize |

Further Reading

Dash, Joan. *The Triumph of Discovery*. New York: Julian Messner, 1991. For young adults. Contains a chapter on Levi-Montalcini.

Holloway, Marguerite. "Finding the Good in the Bad." *Scientific American*, January 1993. Interview with Levi-Montalcini and brief review of her career.

Kahn, Carol. "Tapping the Healers Within." *Omni*, March 1988. Popular article describes the effects of growth factors, including NGF, and their possible importance to medicine.

"Levi-Montalcini, Rita." *Current Biography*, 1989. Concise review of Levi-Montalcini's life and career.

Levi-Montalcini, Rita. *In Praise of Imperfection*. New York: Basic Books, 1988. Levi-Montalcini's autobiography.

Liversidge, Anthony. "Interview: Rita Levi-Montalcini." *Omni*, March 1988. Interesting interview with Levi-Montalcini about her life and the significance of her work.

McGrayne, Sharon. *Nobel Prize Women in Science*. New York: Carol Communications/Birch Lane Press, 1993. For young adults. Contains good chapter on Levi-Montalcini.

Randall, Frederika. "The Heart and Mind of a Genius." *Vogue*, March 1987. Interview with Levi-Montalcini and summary of her life.

Worden, Frederic G., and others. *The Neurosciences: Paths of Discovery*. Cambridge, Mass.: MIT Press, 1975. Contains a chapter in which Levi-Montalcini recalls how she made her discoveries.

Margaret Burbidge helped to describe how chemical elements are formed in stars. She also studies mysterious astronomical objects called quasars. (Courtesy Margaret Burbidge; photo, Pat Gifford)

E. Margaret Burbidge

(1919–)

Billions of years ago, a star blew itself almost out of existence. Most of its matter flew into space as incredibly hot gases. Slowly cooling, the gases drifted away until they were sucked in by the gravity of other stars.

One of those stars was our sun. After being pulled into the solar system, some of the matter from the exploded star, or supernova, eventually became part of Earth and its living things. Astronomer Alan Sandage has said, "Every one of our chemical elements was once inside a star. . . . [All people] are brothers. We came from the same supernova." In fact, many supernovas probably contributed to the elements on Earth.

British-born astronomer Margaret Burbidge is one of the four people who figured out the processes by which chemical elements are created inside stars. With her husband, Geoffrey Burbidge, another astronomer, she has also studied strange starlike objects called quasars. A 1974 article in *Smithsonian* magazine called Margaret Burbidge "probably . . . the foremost woman astronomer in the world."

Eleanor Margaret Peachey was born in Davenport, England, on August 12, 1919. Her father, Stanley Peachey, taught chemistry at the Manchester School of Technology. Her mother, Marjorie, had been one of his few women students. Margaret has one sister, Audrey.

Margaret first became fascinated by the stars when she was just four years old. She became seasick during a rough night crossing of the English Channel. To distract her, her mother took her into the upper bunk of their boat cabin and showed her the stars through a porthole. "They are so beautifully clear at night from a ship," Margaret recalls.

Numbers—the bigger the better—were Margaret's other great interest, once she started school. When she was about 12, her grandfather gave her some books about astronomy. "Suddenly I saw my fascination with the stars . . . linked to my other delight, large numbers," she wrote in a recent autobiographical article. She read, for example, that the star nearest to Earth (except the sun) is 26,000,000,000,000 miles away. "I decided then and there that the occupation I most wanted to engage in 'when I was grown up' was to determine the distances of the stars."

Margaret entered the University College of London (UCL) in 1936 and majored in astronomy. She learned how to set up and use a telescope, but she didn't get to see many stars. Neither London's city lights nor Britain's cloudy weather, she discovered, were good for optical astronomy.

Margaret Peachey graduated from UCL in 1939. She then began work on her Ph.D. project, the study of a kind of star called a B star. As part of this project, Peachey linked a telescope to a device called a spectrograph. Spectrographs let astronomers identify the elements in stars by analyzing the stars' light. Peachey received her Ph.D. in 1943.

After World War II ended in 1945, Peachey wanted to continue her observations with better telescopes and viewing conditions. She applied for a Carnegie Fellowship, which allowed young astronomers to use the telescopes at Mount Wilson Observatory, near Los Angeles, California. She was shocked to be turned down because, she was told, only men were allowed to use the Mount Wilson telescopes.

The path to better telescopes and clearer skies might be blocked for the moment, but other paths in Peachey's life were opening up. While taking a graduate physics course at UCL in the fall of 1947 she met a young physicist named Geoffrey Burbidge. She and Geoff (Jeff), as she called him, quickly became friends. They married on April 2, 1948.

In 1950, Margaret Burbidge obtained a grant to do research at Yerkes Observatory in Williams Bay, Wisconsin, which did allow women astronomers. Geoff, who had also become an astronomer, planned to study at the Harvard University observatory. The Burbidges came to the United States in 1951.

Margaret continued her work on B stars for the next several years. She also studied the structure of galaxies, gigantic star systems that she calls "the building blocks of the universe." (Earth is in the galaxy we call the Milky Way.) She spent part of her time at Yerkes and part at its sister observatory, McDonald Observatory, in Texas. Geoff often worked with her.

In 1953, the Burbidges became interested in the origin of the chemical elements. Some astronomers thought that all the elements had been created when the universe was born. But others, including Fred Hoyle, a famous astronomer who was a friend of the Burbidges, believed that elements are constantly being made inside stars.

A guiding operational principle in my life [is that] . . . if frustrated in one's endeavor by a stone wall or any kind of blockage, one must find a way around— another route toward one's goal.

—Margaret Burbidge

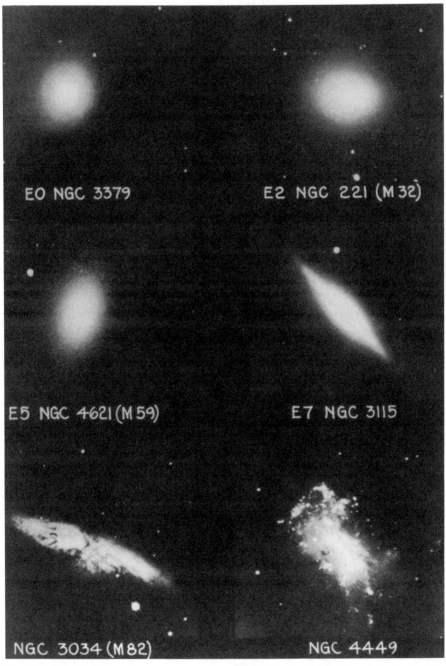

Burbidge studied the giant star systems called galaxies, including galaxies with unusual shapes like these. (Courtesy Yerkes Observatory, University of Chicago)

Hoyle thought elements are created in a series of reactions in which atomic nuclei fuse, or join. Each fusion reaction creates heavier elements than the one before. As science historian Dennis Overbye puts it, "the star becomes layered, like an onion," with each layer containing elements made by a different reaction. When all the fuel for these nuclear reactions is exhausted, the most massive stars end their lives in a violent explosion, becoming supernovas. Some of the heaviest elements are created only in such explosions.

The Burbidges returned to England in mid-1953 and began to work with Hoyle and William Fowler, a nuclear physicist, to refine Hoyle's theory. The four called the new version of the theory the B^2FH theory, from the first letters of their last names. (The Burbidges, who often worked together, were jokingly known to other astronomers as B^2, or "B squared.")

To get more experimental data to support the B^2FH theory, the Burbidges decided to return to the United States in 1955. This time they were determined to work at Mount Wilson, restrictions or not. They obtained grants for the trip, but getting Margaret up to the telescopes was still a challenge. Geoff had to apply for observing time and pretend that Margaret was merely his assistant, even though, as she once said, "Geoff has the ideas. . . . I do the observing." She was not allowed to stay in the astronomers' mountain dormitory. Finally, however, the director of the observatory agreed to let Margaret use the telescopes if she and Geoff lived separately in a nearby cottage.

Margaret photographed the light of stars of different types and ages through a telescope and spectrograph. Analyzing these photos would tell the Burbidges the amounts and kinds of elements in each star. To obtain her photographs, Margaret spent many winter nights in the unheated observatory dome. Her telescope peered out at the sky through an open slit in the dome. She sat on a movable ladder as she guided the telescope to follow whatever star she was studying. Such work would have been too uncomfortable for most people, but Margaret loved it. She stopped it only when pregnancy made climbing too hard.

The Burbidges' daughter, Sarah, was born late in 1956. The paper describing the B^{2}FH theory appeared the following year. This paper listed eight nuclear reactions, each producing different elements, that take place in stars at different stages of their lives. It also showed how elements spewed out by one star could be sucked into another. Dennis Overbye says it "laid out a new view . . . of the galaxy as a dynamic evolving organism, of stars that were . . . an interacting community." Margaret and Geoffrey Burbidge received the Warner Prize in 1959 for the B^{2}FH theory.

After completing their work at Mount Wilson, the Burbidges returned to Yerkes Observatory. There they studied different kinds of galaxies. The University of Chicago, which owns Yerkes and McDonald, made Geoff an associate professor. At the time, however, the university, like many others, had a rule forbidding a husband and wife to work on the same faculty. Margaret therefore was not offered a faculty position, though she did receive a research fellowship. As she has noted, such rules "are always used against the wife."

In contrast, when the University of California set up a new campus at San Diego, it invited both Burbidges to join its faculty. They did so in 1962. Margaret Burbidge was made a full professor of astronomy in 1964.

At San Diego the Burbidges became interested in mysterious objects that had just been discovered—

I felt it was almost sinful to be enjoying astronomy so much, now that it was my job and the source of my livelihood.

—Margaret Burbidge

quasi-stellar radio sources, or quasars for short. Quasars seemed like stars in some ways, but they sent out far more powerful radio waves than any known kind of star. "Quasars are real brainteasers," Margaret Burbidge told an interviewer in 1974. "They are a new class of objects."

When evaluated according to the most commonly held astronomical theories, evidence suggests that the quasars are both very far away and very old—almost as old as the universe itself. The Burbidges suspect that this interpretation may be wrong. They think some quasars may be near galaxies that are not at such enormous distances.

While arguing with other astronomers about what was happening in the farthest reaches of the universe, the Burbidges also became involved in a dispute on Earth. When they visited England in 1971, the head of the Science Research Council (SRC), which controls scientific research in Britain, asked Margaret Burbidge to become director of the Royal Greenwich Observatory. This is Britain's most famous observatory. No woman had ever been its director.

Margaret had doubts, but she finally accepted the position. Geoff was also offered a job at the observatory. Taking a leave of absence from UC–San Diego, the Burbidges moved to England in mid-1972.

Being head of the Royal Greenwich Observatory carried some unusual privileges, such as having an office in a castle. The castle, called Herstmonceux, had been built originally in the 15th century. It included gardens and a moat. Margaret Burbidge soon learned, however, that her castle office did not make her a queen.

First of all, the head of the observatory traditionally had been given the title of astronomer royal—in effect, chief astronomer of England. Burbidge was told, however, that she would not receive this honor. Without explanation, the SRC gave the title to a male astronomer.

Burbidge also faced rebellion within the observatory. Its younger astronomers wanted to move the observatory's 100-inch Isaac Newton Telescope, Britain's largest, out of the country to a spot where the viewing would be better. (Britain would still own and control the telescope.) Burbidge supported this plan, but most of the older astronomers opposed it. They wanted the telescope and the prestige that went with it to stay right where they were.

Geoff learned that, because of the foggy sea air near Herstmonceux, the Newton telescope had been usable for only 600 to 800 hours a year. Telescopes at the best sites in the world, by contrast, could be used about 2,000 hours a year. This information supported the young astronomers' complaints, but it did not change the minds of the "old guard."

Geoff, "never one to suffer fools gladly" as Margaret noted, wrote a blistering letter to the well-known British scientific journal *Nature*. He described the situation at the observatory and called Britain's optical astronomy "third-rate." The head of the SRC saw the letter and summoned the Burbidges to his office. What Margaret calls a "bitter confrontation" followed. Early in 1974, after just 15 months as head of the Greenwich observatory, Margaret Burbidge resigned the post.

Back in the United States, of which she became a citizen in 1977, Burbidge fared better. She became the first woman president of the American Astronomical Society in 1976. In 1978 she was elected to the National Academy of Sciences as well. Finally, in 1981 she became president of the American Association for the Advancement of Science.

During the late 1970s Burbidge also served on the Space Science Board, a group of scientists that advises the National Aeronautics and Space Administration (NASA) about projects in space. She helped to convince NASA that it should launch a telescope facility into space, where viewing would not be obscured by the Earth's atmosphere.

When NASA decided to build such a facility, it made Burbidge part of the team that designed a "faint object spectrograph" to be included in the facility. UC–San Diego was assigned to oversee the building of the spectrograph. The university chancellor created the Center for Astrophysics and Space Sciences to do this and asked Burbidge to head it. She did so until 1988.

The Hubble Space Telescope was finally launched into orbit around the Earth in 1990. Its primary mirror proved to have major problems (which were later fixed), but other devices, including the faint object spectrograph, worked perfectly. Burbidge first used the spectrograph in 1990 to record the far-ultraviolet part of the light of a quasar. She could not have done this with an earthbound telescope because the atmosphere's ozone layer blocks ultraviolet light.

Margaret Burbidge has retired as a university professor, but she still works at UC–San Diego as a research professor. Among other things, she presently studies quasars and the galaxies that seem to be associated with some of them.

When she first used the faint object spectrograph, Burbidge was thrilled, as she puts it, to "see the universe in a new color"—one that could not be seen with the naked eye. But she still remembers most fondly the cold, dark nights of her early years in astronomy. She has written, "I often think about the joys of work in an open [observatory] dome, under the stars, next to the telescope, joys denied to most younger astronomers." Astronomers today, including Burbidge herself, usually work in warm, well-lighted rooms, guiding a telescope with the help of television screens and analyzing starlight with computers. But only the old ways, she feels, made an astronomer truly what 19th-century British poet John Keats called "a watcher of the skies."

Chronology

August 12, 1919	Margaret Peachey born in Davenport, England
1936	enters University College of London
1939	graduates from UCL
1943	receives Ph.D. degree
April 2, 1948	marries Geoffrey Burbidge
1951	begins work at Yerkes Observatory
1953	returns to England; begins work with Fred Hoyle on theory about elements in stars
1955	works at Mount Wilson Observatory
1957	paper on B^{2}FH theory published; Burbidges return to Yerkes
1962	Burbidges move to University of California at San Diego
1964	Margaret Burbidge becomes full professor; studies quasars
1972	becomes head of Royal Greenwich Observatory in England
1974	resigns Greenwich post and returns to San Diego
1981	becomes president of American Association for Advancement of Science
1990	makes first observation with faint object spectrograph

Further Reading

Burbidge, E. Margaret. "Watcher of the Skies." *Annual Review of Astronomy and Astrophysics*, 1994. Long, interesting autobiographical article. Parts are difficult reading.

Green, Timothy. "A Great Woman Astronomer Leaves England—Again." *Smithsonian*, January 1974. Describes controversy at Greenwich Observatory and reviews the Burbidges' lives and work.

Overbye, Dennis. *Lonely Hearts of the Cosmos*. New York: HarperCollins, 1992. Book on modern astronomical discoveries and theories, including material on the B^2FH theory.

"The Stargazer." *Time*, March 20, 1972. Brief review of Margaret Burbidge's career soon after she was chosen to direct the Royal Greenwich Observatory.

Wade, Nicholas. "Astronomy in Britain: Fogged Up by Cloudy Skies and Schisms." *Science*, November 30, 1973. Describes the controversy at the Royal Greenwich Observatory.

Long before most scientists worried about whether carbon dioxide was warming the Earth, Katsuko Saruhashi studied this gas in seawater. She also learned how radioactive fallout from bomb tests spread through the sea and air.
(Courtesy Katsuko Saruhashi)

Katsuko Saruhashi

(1920–   )

Some scientists say that the Earth's future could be a nightmare. Rising temperatures may make the polar ice caps melt. Sea levels could rise, perhaps destroying coastal cities. Whole regions of farmland could turn to desert.

All these things may happen because carbon dioxide (CO_2) in our atmosphere is increasing. Much of this gas comes from natural sources, but most of the increase is probably due to human burning of fossil fuels, such as coal and oil. Carbon dioxide slows the radiation of the sun's heat from Earth's atmosphere into space. Just as the glass of a greenhouse traps heat and makes the inside of the greenhouse warmer than the outside, so extra CO_2 is likely to raise the temperature of the Earth. A rise of even a few degrees could produce disaster.

Scientists disagree about how likely the "greenhouse effect" is to occur and how serious it will be if it does. Concern about it, however, has led chemists and Earth scientists of today to watch CO_2 levels closely. But 45 years ago, no one thought much about CO_2 at all. No one, that is, except a Japanese scientist named Katsuko Saruhashi.

Saruhashi made some of the first studies of CO_2 levels in seawater, which can both take up the gas from and release it into, the air. She also gathered evidence that showed the dangers of radioactive fallout, or dust and debris, produced by nuclear bomb tests. Today she is a leader in seeking greater recognition for women scientists in Japan.

Katsuko Saruhashi was born in Tokyo on March 22, 1920. When she started college at Toho University about 20 years later, Japan was at war. Little science equipment was available at the university. In an attempt to help her find better equipment, one of her professors introduced her to Yasuo Miyake, a government meteorologist, in 1942.

Miyake arranged for Saruhashi to use government laboratory facilities during off hours. More important, he became her adviser, or mentor. "He didn't care if it was a man or a woman," Saruhashi has said. "If a researcher had drive, he would do as much as he could for them."

In those days, most women college graduates with science training—what few there were—became high school teachers. Saruhashi, however, did not want to follow this path after she graduated from Toho in 1943. She was determined to become a research scientist.

Yasuo Miyake was again able to help her. After the war he set up the Geochemical Laboratory as part of the Japanese Transport Ministry's Meteorological Research Institute. The laboratory studied the chemistry of substances naturally found on Earth, including its oceans and atmosphere. Miyake hired Saruhashi to work there as a research assistant.

Around 1950, Miyake recommended that Saruhashi study carbon dioxide in seawater. "Now everyone is concerned about carbon dioxide, but at that time nobody was," she says. The study of CO_2 levels in seawater was so new that Saruhashi had to design her own methods for measuring the gas.

Saruhashi's CO_2 work eventually became her doctoral project. She received her doctor of science degree from Tokyo University in 1957. She was the first woman in the university's history to earn this degree in chemistry.

While she was still studying carbon dioxide, a frightening event captured Saruhashi's attention. It involved the test of a hydrogen bomb, a nuclear weapon that was developed in the early 1950s. Unlike the atomic bomb, which had grown indirectly from Lise Meitner's insight about atomic fission, the hydrogen bomb produces its tremendous energy from fusion, or joining, of atomic nuclei. Margaret Burbidge was studying this same kind of reaction in stars.

The United States tested a hydrogen bomb by exploding it on the tiny Pacific island of Bikini on March 1, 1954. Government observers tried to make sure no one was near the test site, but they failed to spot a little Japanese tuna-fishing boat called the *Fifth Lucky Dragon*.

The crew of the *Lucky Dragon* were anything but lucky. Although they were about 100 miles from Bikini, wind blowing from the test site showered them with fine, white dust.

The *Lucky Dragon* tells us not only her tragic history, but also the fate of humanity in the nuclear age. We anticipate the total abolishment of nuclear weapons and the establishment of a world without war. *Lucky Dragon* must continue to be the symbol of world peace and peace education.

—Professor Yasuo Miyake, Katsuko Saruhashi's mentor

The members of the 23-man crew most heavily exposed to this deadly snow soon showed signs of severe radiation poisoning. One of them died in September 1954.

Radioactive fallout from bomb tests became known as the "ashes of death." The heaviest particles fell near the test site, but scientists, including Saruhashi, soon learned that lighter particles were carried high into the atmosphere and spread around the world. They fell to earth again in rain and snow. If they landed in the sea, ocean currents carried them further distances. If they fell on land, soil took them up. They could be absorbed by plants and then by animals that ate the plants. Humans took them in with their food.

Soon after the Bikini test, the Japanese government asked Miyake's geochemical laboratory to monitor levels of radioactivity in rain throughout Japan. Saruhashi also measured radioactivity in seawater, both off the coasts of Japan and near the bomb test site. She says that she and her coworkers were the first group in the world to make such measurements. She found that fallout from the test took about a year and a half to reach Japan in seawater.

Nuclear bomb testing slowly increased during the late 1950s and early 1960s. So did worldwide concern about the dangers of fallout. People who wanted to end bomb testing cited the data gathered by Saruhashi and others, which showed how far fallout could spread. Global protests finally persuaded the United States and the Soviet Union to sign the Limited Test Ban Treaty in 1963. The treaty required that all future bomb tests be done underground. That way, fallout would not escape into the atmosphere.

During the 1960s, Saruhashi continued to study radioactive matter in both seawater and the atmosphere. Such material came from continuing bomb tests (France and the People's Republic of China were still conducting aboveground tests) and also from sources such as nuclear power plants. Saruhashi carried out some of her research at the

Scripps Institution of Oceanography in La Jolla, California. She found that by 1964, levels of certain radioactive compounds in the sea off California were about the same as those she had noted near Japan 10 years earlier. This suggested that after 10 years, surface water from the western and eastern parts of the North Pacific had mixed completely. By 1969, Saruhashi discovered, the compounds had spread throughout the Pacific. She found them in both surface and deep waters.

Saruhashi also went on with her studies of carbon dioxide. Her later studies focused on the movement of the gas between the atmosphere and the oceans. This movement is important because there is about 60 times more CO_2 dissolved in seawater than in the air. If the seas absorbed more CO_2 from the air than they released into it, they might help to prevent the greenhouse effect. Unfortunately, Saruhashi found that the opposite is true. At least in the Pacific Ocean, seawater releases about twice as much CO_2 as it absorbs.

Other environmental problems attracted Saruhashi's attention as well. In 1984, for example, she reported an investigation of acid rain. Like the buildup of CO_2, acid rain is thought to arise mainly from the products of burning fossil fuels and other forms of air pollution. The acid in the rain can damage buildings, plants, and aquatic life.

Saruhashi measured levels of acid in rain over Tokyo. She then compared her results with those Yasuo Miyake had obtained in a similar study in 1939. She was surprised to discover that the levels were about the same, even though air pollution had increased greatly during the 45 years between the two studies. She suspects this happened because natural particles in the air over Japan can more successfully neutralize the kind of acid produced by burning oil, which is the main kind today, than they could the kind produced by burning coal, which was more common in the 1930s.

Today Katsuko Saruhashi is the executive director of the Geochemistry Research Association in Tokyo. Yasuo Miyake founded this organization in 1972 to help spread information related to the chemistry of materials in the earth. It also sponsors research on the peaceful uses of nuclear power.

Saruhashi's pioneering work in geochemistry has brought her many awards. She was elected to the Science Council of Japan, the country's "parliament of science," in 1980. She was the council's first woman member. In 1981 she received the Avon Special Prize for Women for her "effort to research the peaceful use of nuclear power and raise up the status of women scientists." She won the Miyake Prize for geochemistry (established by Yasuo Miyake in 1972) in 1985; to date, no other woman has received this honor. Most recently, in 1993, she won the Tanaka Prize from the Society of Sea Water Sciences. She is an honorary member of both the Geochemical Society of Japan and the Oceanographical Society of Japan.

There are many women who have the ability to become great scientists. I would like to see the day when women can contribute to science and technology on an equal footing with men.

—Katsuko Saruhashi

Even more important to Saruhashi than the awards she has won is the prize she has established for other women scientists. The prize grew out of money that friends and coworkers raised for her when she retired as director of the Geochemical Laboratory in 1980, after she had held the post for a year. The money amounted to 5,000,000 yen, or about $50,000. Instead of keeping the money for herself, Saruhashi used it to establish a group called the Association for the Bright Future of Women Scientists. One of the group's aims is to publicize the "gloomy conditions" under which most women scientists in Japan work. Saruhashi had started an earlier women scientists' organization, the Society of Japanese Women Scientists, in 1958.

Saruhashi also used her gift money to establish the Saruhashi Prize in 1980. This prize is awarded yearly to a Japanese woman 50 years old or younger who has made important contributions to the natural sciences. "I wanted to highlight the capabilities of women scientists," Saruhashi says. The cash amount of the award is fairly small—300,000 yen, or about $3,000. The recognition the award provides is its chief value.

Saruhashi has said of the recipients of the Saruhashi Prize, "Each winner has been not only a successful researcher but . . . a wonderful human being as well. They have become role models for those who will follow in their footsteps." It is obvious that the same can be said of Katsuko Saruhashi.

Chronology

March 22, 1920	Katsuko Saruhashi born in Tokyo
1942	meets Yasuo Miyake
1943	graduates from Toho University
1945	begins work at the Geochemical Laboratory
1950s	studies carbon dioxide in seawater
March 1, 1954	United States tests hydrogen bomb at Bikini

1957	receives doctor of science degree from Tokyo University
1954–69	Saruhashi measures radioactive compounds in seawater and atmosphere
1958	establishes Society of Japanese Women Scientists
1970s–80s	studies acid rain and other environmental problems
1979	becomes director of Geochemical Laboratory
1980	elected to Science Council of Japan; retires as director of Geochemical Laboratory; establishes Association for the Bright Future of Women Scientists and the Saruhashi Prize
1981	wins Avon Special Prize for Women
1985	wins Miyake Prize
1993	wins Tanaka Prize

Further Reading

Normile, Dennis. "A Prize of One's Own." *Science*, April 16, 1993. Concise description of Saruhashi's career and the Saruhashi Prize.

Richards, Francis A. "A Note on Japanese Women in Science." *Scientific Bulletin*, Oct.–Dec. 1981. Brief description of Saruhashi's career, the Society of Japanese Women Scientists, and the Saruhashi Prize.

"The Science of Equality." *Look Japan*, September 1990. Describes the Saruhashi Prize and briefly profiles women who won it during the 1980s.

"The Science of Equality." *Look Japan*, September 1990. Describes the Saruhashi Prize and briefly profiles women who won it during the 1980s.

Rosalind Franklin's X-ray photographs of deoxyribonucleic acid (DNA), which carries inherited information in "coded" form, provided vital clues to the chemical's structure. (Courtesy King's College Archives, University of London)

Rosalind Elsie Franklin

(1920-1958)

The picture, an X made of evenly spaced black blobs, didn't look very exciting. But to those who understood it, it offered a key to one of life's most important secrets: how living things pass on traits to their offspring.

The woman who took the picture was Rosalind Franklin. She made it by shining a beam of X rays through DNA (deoxyribonucleic acid), the chief chemical that carries inherited information. The pattern made by the reflected X rays suggested how the complex DNA molecule is constructed.

Franklin herself did not discover the secret of DNA's structure. Perhaps, if circumstances had been different, she might have. As it was, her photo provided the breakthrough piece of information that allowed others to do so.

Franklin's X-ray photographs of DNA were only one of her achievements. Her discoveries about the molecules of carbon led indirectly to the creation of strong, lightweight materials used in experimental cars and planes. She also did pioneering work on the structure of viruses, which can cause devastating diseases.

Rosalind Elsie Franklin was born in London on July 25, 1920. Like Rita Levi-Montalcini and Lise Meitner, she belonged to a well-to-do Jewish family. Her father, Ellis, was a banker. Muriel, her mother, devoted herself to the needs of her husband and five children. Rosalind was the second of those children.

When Rosalind wanted to go to college, she ran into the same problem that Meitner and Levi-Montalcini had. Her father, like theirs, thought higher education made women unhappy. He suggested that she do volunteer work instead.

Rosalind responded, as she would always do when someone tried to block her, with passionate opposition. She had known since the age of 15 that she wanted to be a scientist. Her sharp mind loved the clear logic and precise answers found in the physical sciences. Faced with such determination, her father, like the fathers of Meitner and Levi-Montalcini, gave in.

Rosalind Franklin entered Newnham College, one of the women's colleges in Cambridge University, in 1938. In a letter home she described it as "rather like a boarding school." Showing the dedication that marked all her working life, Franklin often spent more than eight hours a day in the college laboratories. She graduated in 1941.

Britain was at war during those years, and Franklin wanted to help her country. She quit graduate school after less than a year. In 1942 the government assigned her to be assistant research officer at the British Coal Utilization Research Association (CURA). This organization looked for better ways to use coal as a fuel. It also sponsored research on the basic nature of coal and other forms of carbon.

Franklin worked for CURA from 1942 to 1946. Some of her research there became the project for her Ph.D., which she earned in 1945. Her work on the structure of carbon molecules, according to one professor, "brought order into a field which had previously been in chaos."

Franklin was well on her way to an established science career by the time the war was over, but she wanted to try something new. She went to France in 1947 and began working at the government chemical research laboratory in Paris. She remained there until the end of 1950.

Those who knew her say that Franklin's years in Paris were the happiest of her life. She enjoyed not only her research but also an active social life with her coworkers. The group liked to gather after work at nearby cafés and picnic together in the countryside on weekends.

At the French laboratory, Franklin learned how to perform X-ray crystallography. In this technique a beam of X rays is passed through a crystal. The atoms and molecules in a crystal are arranged in regular, three-dimensional patterns. Different substances form crystals with different patterns.

When an X-ray beam is sent through a crystal, some rays in the beam bounce off the atoms in the crystal. Others hit nothing and pass through. As a result, the beam is broken up. On leaving the crystal, the scattered rays strike photographic film and leave characteristic marks. These X-ray photographs can reveal clues about the three-dimensional arrangement of atoms inside a molecule.

Using X-ray crystallography, Franklin divided forms of carbon and carbon compounds into two groups. One group changed easily into graphite (the form of carbon in pencil "leads") when heated. The other did not. Substances in the two groups had different qualities. Some of Franklin's work in France helped to lay the foundation for the development of lightweight, high-strength carbon fibers. Such fibers are used today in experimental cars and planes.

Franklin became especially skillful in making X-ray photos of amorphous substances, materials that did not form obvious crystals. Many substances in the bodies of living things are amorphous, but scientists were beginning to realize that X-ray crystallography could help them figure out the molecular structure of these complex compounds. The structure of biological molecules has a lot to do with the way these molecules function in living things.

Rosalind Franklin was eager to try her crystallography skill on biological molecules. In 1950 King's College, a part of the University of London, offered her a chance to do just that. John Randall, the head of the biophysics laboratory at King's, told Franklin that she would be working on DNA—one of the most important biological molecules of all.

Scientists knew that DNA carried hereditary information, but they didn't know how. Many suspected that the secret of DNA's function lay in its structure. Scientists of this time knew that the DNA molecule was made of multiple copies of four kinds of smaller molecules called bases. The bases were attached to a chain made up of sugar and phosphate (a compound containing the element phosphorus). No one knew, however, exactly how these molecules were arranged within the DNA molecule. Did they form a straight chain, or was the chain twisted into a spiral, or helix, like a curving staircase or a screw? If the chain did twist, was the phosphate-sugar "backbone" on the inside or the outside? Did each DNA molecule consist of just one chain of phosphate and bases, or did two or even three chains exist side by side? Randall hoped that Franklin could make X-ray photographs that would help the DNA research group at King's answer these questions.

Franklin began working at King's College in January 1951. Unfortunately, she and Maurice Wilkins, the DNA group's leader, disliked each other intensely almost on sight. Part of the problem may have been a misunderstanding about Franklin's exact position in the lab. Part may have been that Franklin was a strong-minded woman.

Most of the trouble may have happened simply because Franklin and Wilkins were such very different people. Franklin was outspoken and loved a good argument. Wilkins, on the other hand, disliked arguing. He told Anne Sayre, Franklin's friend and biographer, "She [Franklin] denounced, and this made it quite impossible as far as I was concerned to have a civil conversation. I simply had to walk away." Raymond Gosling, a graduate student who worked with Franklin at King's, confirmed, "You had to argue strongly with Rosalind if she thought you were wrong, whereas Maurice [Wilkins] would simply shut up."

Whatever its causes, the conflict between Wilkins and Franklin harmed the work of both. It meant that both, but especially Franklin, had no one of their own rank to talk to about their ideas. Such discussions can help scientists recognize mistakes and give them new insights.

Two other scientists who were trying to discover the structure of DNA, by contrast, worked together very well. They were at Cambridge University, from which Franklin herself had graduated earlier. The younger was James Watson, an American who was then only about 24 years old. The older was a British scientist, Francis Crick.

Watson, especially, was sure that DNA's structure would prove extremely important to biology. He saw the attempt to find that structure as a three-way race between himself and Crick, Wilkins and the others at King's College, and an American scientist, Linus Pauling. Pauling had become famous for discovering the structure of other biological molecules. Most of the other "contestants," however—and above all, Franklin—never felt that they were in a race. Even Crick said later that

That Rosalind lacked for a friend and confidant, while everyone else involved in the DNA race was amply supplied with both, comes . . . to explain a great deal.

—Anne Sayre, Franklin's biographer and friend

"the only person who thought it was a race was Jim [Watson]."

Wilkins's group had already taken some X-ray photographs of a crystalline form of DNA. Franklin took better ones. She also found a way to make DNA take up water, which produced a form of DNA that gave X-ray photos different from those of the crystalline kind. No one had made this "wet" form of DNA before. To distinguish it from the crystalline or A form, Franklin called the new type the B form.

Based on her X-ray photos, Franklin concluded that the chains in the B form of DNA, at least, had the shape of a helix. She believed that the phosphate backbone was on the outside of each chain. The bases were inside, forming the steps in the "staircase." She wasn't sure whether there were two, three, or four chains in each molecule.

Franklin described her conclusions in a talk in November 1951. Several scientists from other universities, including James Watson, attended the talk. Watson did not take notes, however, and he apparently did not listen very carefully, either. For example, he thought that Franklin did not realize that her photographs showed that the B form of DNA was a helix, but her notes for the talk show clearly that she did.

Franklin, in turn, seems not to have recognized how important the B form of DNA was. Beginning in the spring of 1952, she worked primarily with the A form, perhaps because it gave sharper X-ray pictures. But in fact, according to Sayre, an X-ray beam bounced off several DNA molecules at once in the A form. In the B form, by contrast, the water separated the molecules from each other. The X-ray beam therefore reflected off only one molecule at a time, providing a more accurate picture.

Franklin did not ignore the B form entirely. In May 1952 she made a photograph of it, using an extra-long exposure. This photo showed a very clear X-shaped pattern, which

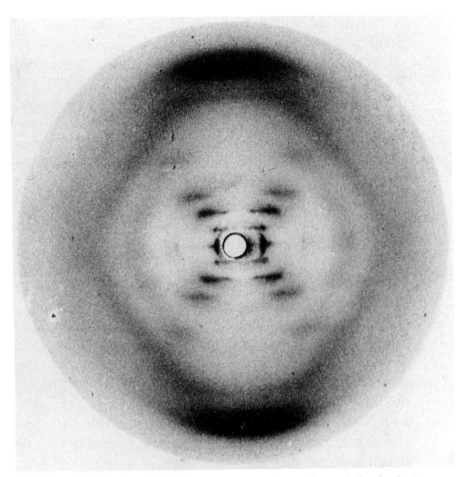

Franklin's X-ray photograph of the B form of DNA showed clearly that the DNA molecule was shaped like a helix, or spiral. (Courtesy King's College Archives, University of London)

indicated that the B form was a helix. But Franklin simply put the photo in a drawer and went back to the A form.

In February 1953, Franklin returned to the B form of DNA, but by then she was too late. The race she did not know she was competing in was heading toward the finish line. It had been pushed there by events that took place on January 30, when James Watson paid a visit to King's College.

Watson and Wilkins had become friends, but Watson and Franklin disliked each other. On this visit they had an angry confrontation. Hurrying out of Franklin's lab, Watson met Wilkins, and the two sympathized with each other about the difficulties of working with Franklin. Then Wilkins mentioned that Franklin had found a second, "wet" form of DNA: the B form. Watson asked what it looked like, and Wilkins—without asking Franklin's permission—showed him the photo that she had taken in May 1952 and then ignored.

The picture was a revelation to Watson. "My mouth fell open and my pulse began to race," he wrote later. He hurried back to Cambridge to tell Crick about it. Crick had not known about the B form. Watson had heard about it in Franklin's 1951 lecture, but apparently he had not remembered it.

Franklin's photo provided experimental evidence for ideas that Watson and Crick were already beginning to have about DNA's structure. Eventually they might have gotten the same evidence by taking X-ray photos themselves, but they lacked the experience and equipment to do this easily. If they had had to spend time making their own photographs, someone else, perhaps Franklin herself, might have figured out DNA's structure before they did.

There was nothing wrong in Watson and Crick using information that came from another scientist. Sayre and some others feel that the two treated Franklin badly, however, in that they did not ask her permission to see her unpublished work. They also never fully acknowledged its importance.

Franklin's work was unquestionably important in helping Watson and Crick work out the structure of DNA, but just as unquestionably their imaginations went beyond it. Crick realized that the two DNA chains, each in the shape of a helix, coiled in opposite directions. The molecule thus looked the same from either end. Watson, in turn, guessed that the bases inside the chains always joined each other in pairs. Adenine always paired with thymine, and cytosine paired with guanine. These two ideas were the vital missing pieces of the DNA puzzle that neither Franklin nor anyone else had been able to discover. Watson and Crick published a short paper describing their ideas in *Nature*, a well-known British science journal, on April 25, 1953.

As Watson had suspected, DNA's structure explained how the chemical carries genetic information. Francis Crick wrote in a letter to his son,

It is like a code. If you are given one set of letters you can write down the others. Now we believe that the D.N.A. *is* a code. The order of the bases (the letters) makes one gene different from another gene (just as one page of print is different from another).

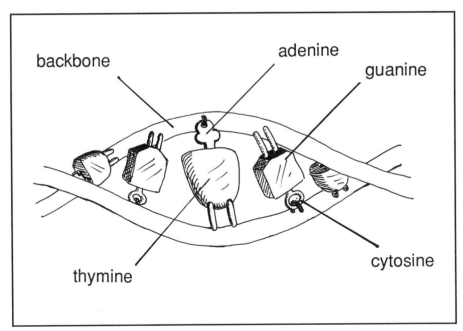

The DNA molecule is actually a double helix. Bases (adenine, thymine, guanine, and cytosine) join in pairs inside the two spiral-shaped phosphate "backbones." (Courtesy Katherine MacFarlane)

The symmetrical structure of the DNA molecule also explains how DNA passes on its information. When a cell prepares to divide, the paired chains in its DNA molecules come apart like a zipper unzipping. Half of each chain is then rebuilt from free bases in the cell. The result is two complete copies of the cell's DNA, one for each daughter cell. When two living things mate, their sex cells (egg and sperm) unite, and the DNA in them is passed on to the resulting offspring.

Rosalind Franklin never learned how much her X-ray photograph had contributed to Watson and Crick's discovery. By the time their paper appeared, she was no longer working on DNA. Frustrated by the continuing conflict at King's, she moved in March to Birkbeck College, another college in the University of London, and took up a different project.

Franklin's work at Birkbeck focused on the tobacco mosaic virus (TMV), which causes a plant disease. Viruses are on the border between living and nonliving things. They can reproduce only when they get inside a cell and use the cell's chemical machinery. Outside the cell, they can exist in the form of crystals. This meant that Franklin could use X-ray crystallography to study them. Viruses were just beginning to be studied in detail in the early 1950s, and TMV was the first to be studied by X-ray crystallography.

Franklin worked out a general plan for TMV's structure, a great stride for the time. TMV is made up of RNA (a chemical similar to DNA) and protein. Franklin showed that the virus's RNA, which carried its genetic information, was a helix, much like DNA. A model of her

The kind of single-mindedness that she had made her an absolutely first-class experimental worker.

—Aaron Klug, who worked with Franklin at Birkbeck

TMV structure was exhibited at the World's Fair in Brussels, Belgium, in 1957.

During Franklin's first three years at Birkbeck, according to Anne Sayre, "everything that she put her hand to went right." But in 1956, pain forced Franklin to go to a doctor, and she learned that she had cancer. All attempts to treat it failed, and Franklin died on April 16, 1958. She was only 37 years old.

In 1962, James Watson, Francis Crick, and Maurice Wilkins received the Nobel Prize in physiology or medicine for their work on the structure of DNA. There was no question of Franklin's receiving a prize, because the Nobel Prize is never awarded after a person's death. But what if Franklin had lived? The prize is never divided among more than three scientists. Watson and Crick certainly would have won. But would Franklin have replaced Wilkins? Would both have been left out? Or would they have been given a joint prize in chemistry instead of medicine? No one knows.

In any case, most scientists who knew Franklin held her in high esteem. J. D. Bernal, who headed the Birkbeck laboratory, wrote of her, "As a scientist Miss Franklin was distinguished by extreme clarity and perfection in everything she undertook. Her photographs are among the most beautiful X-ray photographs . . . ever taken."

Chronology

July 25, 1920	Rosalind Franklin born in London
1938	enters Newnham College, Cambridge
1941	graduates from Newnham
1942–46	works for Coal Utilization Research Association

1945	receives Ph.D. from Cambridge
1947–50	does carbon research in Paris; learns X-ray crystallography
January 1951	begins work on DNA at King's College
November 1951	gives talk stating that B form of DNA is a helix
1952	works mostly on A form; takes beautiful picture of B form
January 30, 1953	James Watson sees Franklin's picture of B form
February 1953	Franklin returns to work on B form; Watson and Crick work out DNA structure
March 1953	Franklin transfers to Birkbeck College
April 25, 1953	Watson and Crick's paper about DNA structure published
1953–57	Franklin works on tobacco mosaic virus
April 16, 1958	Franklin dies
1962	Watson, Crick, and Wilkins receive Nobel Prize for work on structure of DNA

Further Reading

Bernstein, Jeremy. *Experiencing Science.* New York: E.P. Dutton, 1978. Contains a chapter evaluating Franklin's contribution to discovery of the structure of DNA.

Crick, Francis. *What Mad Pursuit.* New York: Basic Books, 1988. Memoir about the discovery of the structure of DNA includes some references to Franklin.

Judson, Horace Freeland. *The Eighth Day of Creation.* New York: Simon and Schuster, 1979. Detailed account of the DNA "race" contains objective evaluation of Franklin's role. Somewhat difficult reading.

————. "The Legend of Rosalind Franklin." *Science Digest*, January 1986. Points out inaccuracies in both positive and negative presentations of Franklin.

Klug, Aaron. "Rosalind Franklin and the Discovery of the Structure of DNA." *Nature*, August 24, 1968. Positive evaluation of Franklin by scientist who worked with her at Birkbeck College.

McGrayne, Sharon. *Nobel Prize Women in Science*. New York: Carol Communications/Birch Lane Press, 1993. For young adults. Includes excellent chapter on Franklin.

Sayre, Anne. *Rosalind Franklin and DNA*. New York: Norton, 1975. Full-length biography of Franklin by a personal friend, strongly biased in Franklin's favor.

Watson, James D. *The Double Helix*. New York: New American Library/Signet, 1959. Lively but biased memoir of the DNA "race." Contains very negative portrait of Franklin that her supporters say is inaccurate.

R. Rajalakshmi developed nutritious diets that were suited to the culture of India and poor families' budgets. (Courtesy V. Ramakrishnan)

R. Rajalakshmi

(1926–)

The gaunt-faced Indian mother wrapped her young son protectively in the folds of her sari. The boy's stomach bulged, but his matchstick-thin arms showed that this swelling was caused by too little food, not too much. His hair was thin and his skin scaly and wrinkled, as if he were an old man trapped in a child's body. The child was six years old, but he was no taller than a healthy child of four.

"Your son is malnourished," the clinic nurse told the mother. "What food do you give him?"

"A cup of weak tea in the morning. Then a piece of white bread at noon and rice at night, with a little fish or coconut sometimes." The mother sighed. "That is all we have."

"Well, he needs more protein," the nurse said briskly. She consulted a large book in front of her. "He should have meat at least twice a week, and of course milk, eggs. . . ."

The mother stared at her. Meat? Milk? Eggs? Few people in India—and no poor people—ever ate such foods.

Today such a scene would be unlikely to occur. Health care workers no longer treat malnutrition in places like India by prescribing a diet designed for a different culture. Instead, they recommend foods that are inexpensive, available locally, and easy to prepare. This practical approach grew out of the work of several Indian scientists, among whom a woman named R. Rajalakshmi was a pioneer.

R. Rajalakshmi was born in 1926 in Quilon, part of the Indian state of Kerala. As a child she was called Lakshmi, after her grandmother. Her father was named G. S. Ramaswami Iyer. (In southern India, the first initial before a person's name traditionally is the first letter of the name of the place where the person was born. The second initial is the first letter of the name of the person's father.) He worked in the postal audit office in the city of Madras, and Lakshmi grew up there. He often brought books home from the library so his family could read and discuss them. Lakshmi's mother, Meenakshi, was a fine cook and loved music and folk dancing. Because her mother was often ill, Lakshmi helped to raise her four younger brothers and sisters. She also had an older brother and sister.

At home, Lakshmi was so quiet that one of her relatives called her "clay cat." (Real cats are quiet, but they meow sometimes. A clay cat would make no sound at all.) But her silence hid a rebellious spirit. When she entered school at age five, for example, she decided to change her name by adding to it the prefix *Raja*, which means "royal." She has used it in this form ever since. Except for an initial, R., it is the only name she uses. (The R., which originally stood for her father's name, now stands for the name of her husband, Ramakrishnan. She has dropped the initial that stands for her place of birth.)

Rajalakshmi's rebellion was combined with intelligence and determination. She tricked school officials into letting her skip 8th grade by telling them she had completed the grade "in private study." "Private study" meant that she had read all her older sister's 8th-grade textbooks the previous summer! Eventually the officials caught on, but she was doing so well in her 9th-grade classes that they let her stay.

Rajalakshmi entered Wadia College, in Poona, in 1941. In her first year she was one of only six girls in a class of 200. She majored in mathematics and graduated in 1945.

After college Rajalakshmi became a teacher in Kancheepuram, in southeastern India. Besides her regular classes, she taught Sunday classes at an industrial school for Harijans, or "untouchables." These people belonged to India's lowest caste, or hereditary social class. Rajalakshmi shocked some of her acquaintances by sharing meals with her Harijan students.

While Rajalakshmi was in Kancheepuram, she became friends with a young man named C. V. Ramakrishnan. He had been her classmate at Wadia College, but they had never spoken to each other there. She got to know him only when he visited his family in Kancheepuram. They married in June 1951.

Rajalakshmi was thrilled when India became independent from Britain in 1947. "It was sheer joy to see the national flag flying," she has written. But her excitement turned to sorrow only a few months later, when India's great pacifist leader, Mahatma Gandhi, was assassinated. "It meant the loss of an idol or ideal. I had never felt such profound grief at any other time before or after." Gandhi's murder not only deprived India of a great man but showed that his belief that nonviolence could turn away violence was not always correct.

After three years in Kancheepuram, Rajalakshmi returned to Madras and enrolled in 1948 in the Lady Willingdon Training College, a teacher training school. As part of her studies, she watched experienced teachers at work. The teacher from whom she gained the most was Miss Nathaniel, who taught high school mathematics. Miss Nathaniel did not simply explain mathematical theorems to her students and show how the theorems were proved. Instead, she helped the students formulate and prove the theorems for themselves, guiding them with "thought-provoking questions" at each step. Rajalakshmi later used this method in the school and college classes she taught.

Rajalakshmi completed her teacher training in 1949. She went on to earn a master's degree in philosophy in 1953 from Banaras Hindu University. She also took courses focused in psychology, sociology, and social psychology. She and Ramakrishnan later studied in Canada. She received her Ph.D. from McGill University, in Montreal, early in 1958.

Ramakrishnan became head of the biochemistry department at the University of Baroda early in 1955. Rajalakshmi often worked with him and helped his students plan and write up their research. Even after she obtained her Ph.D., however, the university officials would not hire her because they did not consider her fully qualified as a nutritionist or biochemist.

Baroda University finally hired Rajalakshmi in 1964, after she and Ramakrishnan were almost lured away by attractive positions elsewhere. She became part of the university's foods and nutrition department, where she remained until 1967. She then joined her husband in the department of biochemistry. She became a full professor there in 1976.

While she was trying to advance her career, Rajalakshmi was also raising her son, Venki, and daughter, Lali. Combining teaching, research, and child care was anything but easy. When Lali was a baby, for example, Rajalakshmi once put her in a playpen in the yard while she sat next to the child and studied. Lali, as independent as her mother, protested this arrangement loudly. When Rajalakshmi tried letting Lali wander freely, the little girl played with her research papers. Finally Rajalakshmi found a unique solution to the problem.

She sat inside the playpen with her papers, while Lali played happily nearby!

Rajalakshmi had been interested in nutrition, especially that of mothers and children, ever since high school. Around 1963 she helped to organize a course in applied nutrition that was sponsored by UNICEF and the Indian government. The course educated officials about India's most important nutritional problems and possible solutions to them. Here her varied academic background proved very useful. She and Ramakrishnan often worked together on nutrition research projects, just as Margaret and Geoffrey Burbidge did in astronomy.

When Rajalakshmi began teaching nutrition courses at Baroda, she discovered that most teachers of such courses used textbooks that had been written mainly in the United States or Europe. The books recommended foods commonly eaten in Western cultures, such as orange juice, milk, beef, and eggs. Such foods were either unavailable or very expensive in India. Rajalakshmi planned courses that focused instead on cooking methods that were familiar to most Indian people.

Rajalakshmi soon learned that this lack of understanding was not limited to the classroom. In the early 1960s she helped to manage a nutrition program sponsored partly by the United Nations. She was unhappy to learn that the program's leaders planned to recommend foods that were not likely to be affordable or even available in India. She also questioned the quantities of nutrients the program recommended. For example, she thought people could get by with less protein than the program sponsors believed.

Rajalakshmi decided to start the program over from scratch. She began by finding out what healthy people of the Indian middle and upper classes ate. Then she studied which cheap and easily available foods might provide the same nutrients to poorer people. Because processed foods were expensive, she limited herself mostly to plant foods that were grown locally and could be prepared with simple cooking equipment. Such an approach might seem obvious, but Rajalakshmi says that it "seemed quite original and almost unique at the time."

The children of India's poorest families needed the most help with their diets. Such children were often malnourished even before birth. Rajalakshmi noted in 1982 that many of India's poor children died before age five. Many poor children suffered from diarrhea, which further cut down on the amount of nutrition their bodies could retain. They became so weak from this and other illnesses that they could not respond to their families' affection. The children therefore grew up stunted in psychological as well as physical growth. They often appeared to be less intelligent than they really were. Luckily, Rajalakshmi found that these mental problems decreased greatly when the children's physical health and nutrition improved.

Rajalakshmi studied poor children's diets in Trivandrum, a coastal city, and Madurai, a city more inland. In Trivandrum, people had traditionally eaten fish and rice. But Rajalakshmi learned that more and more fish were being exported, which left less for the local people. More land was being used to raise coconuts for export and less to grow rice for food. People subsituted tapioca, a starchy food, for the more nutritious rice. These changes, Rajalakshmi wrote, "resulted in the poor man's diet becoming poorer." Instead of traditional breakfast foods

> Children [in city slums] may be obliged to grow up huddled in shacks . . . or, worse, on roadside pavements, without . . . drinking or bath water, sanitary [bathroom] facilities and amidst stagnant pools of . . . slop water.
>
> —R. Rajalakshmi

Many Indian mothers and children, like this pair, are healthy and eat good diets. Children in poor families, however, may suffer from lack of grains, vegetables, and other nutritious foods. (Courtesy India Tourist Office)

such as fermented rice, families had only weak coffee or tea. For lunch and dinner, most had rice or tapioca as a main dish, with a little fish or coconut.

Poor families in Madurai had a slightly better diet. More of them than in Trivandrum ate traditional breakfasts that contained some nourishment. Lunch and dinner consisted of rice or hot cereal plus a curry made of vegetables or, occasionally, meat.

Beginning in 1965, Rajalakshmi and her coworkers set up several programs to improve poor children's diets and educate poor families about nutrition. For example, they told the families to serve four meals a day (breakfast, lunch, tea in the afternoon, and dinner). This was a good idea because young children do not eat very much in a single meal.

In their first program, the nutrition workers fed the children a balanced diet that included cereal, legumes (nutritious plants related to peas and peanuts), vegetables, and buttermilk. A later program simplified the diet, while maintaining its high nutritional content, by serving a traditional Indian dish called dhokla. Dhokla includes grain, legumes, and leafy vegetables. The grain and legumes provide protein, and the vegetables add vitamins and minerals. Adding lime (calcium hydroxide) to the fermented batter used to make dhokla enriched the diet in calcium.

In order to increase the chances that children would eat well at home, the workers gave each family packets containing a mixture of roasted ground wheat and bengalgram, a legume. The workers asked the mothers to make porridge (soft cereal something like oatmeal) with the mixture and serve it in the morning and evening with a little milk and a spoonful of oil enriched with vitamin A, which was also provided.

Rajalakshmi and her coworkers found that these programs helped preschool children almost double their food intake. Dhokla and other one-dish meals were the most helpful. When mothers followed the program's advice, their children's growth rate began to match that of upperclass children.

Today, Rajalakshmi says, "many of the ideas I advanced during my

I have generally not compromised on principles, and have stood up for what I consider right either at home or outside.

—R. Rajalakshmi

research career . . . which were received somewhat skeptically by some scientists in the field are now accepted as commonplace." These include the ideas that people do not need as much protein as had been thought and that diets made entirely of plant food can provide all needed nutrients. Scientists now also accept Rajalakshmi's finding that close ties between mother and child are as important as good food in preventing the brain-damaging effects of early childhood malnutrition. She feels that her special contribution to science has been a "capacity for insight and intuition which made [me] think of common-sense solutions to seemingly complex problems."

Rajalakshmi took over Ramakrishnan's position as head of the Baroda biochemistry department in 1984. She says that heading the department was "not an easy job." Both she and Ramakrishnan retired from the university early in 1986. The Indian Council of Medical Research invited Rajalakshmi to head one of its six centers for nutrition research and training, but a stroke she suffered late in 1986 forced her to give up this post. Her main interest at present is the traditional Indian spiritual discipline of yoga.

Rajalakshmi also continues her concern with the world's poor and hungry people, especially mothers and children. As she said at a 1982 conference on child nutrition, "It is time we realised that ultimately the future of this planet earth and the beings it houses depends on the promotion of the welfare of all."

Chronology

1926	R. Rajalakshmi born in Quilon, Kerala, India
1941	enters Wadia College in Poona

1945	graduates from Wadia College
1945–48	teaches science in Kancheepuram
1947	India becomes independent from Britain
1948	Gandhi assassinated; Rajalakshmi enrolls in Lady Willingdon Training College
1949	completes teacher training
1951	marries C. V. Ramakrishnan
1953	receives master's degree from Benaras University
1955	Ramakrishnan becomes head of biochemistry department at University of Baroda
1958	Rajalakshmi earns Ph.D. from McGill
early 1960s	helps to manage and revise nutrition program sponsored by UNICEF and other international organizations
1964–67	works in foods and nutrition department of Baroda University; designs programs to improve nutrition of poor children
1967-84	works with Ramakrishnan in biochemistry department; continues studies of nutrition
1976	becomes full professor in biochemistry
1984–86	heads Baroda biochemistry department
1986	retires from Baroda; has stroke

Further Reading

Rajalakshmi, R. *Applied Nutrition*. Janpath, Delhi: IBH/Oxford, 1984. Difficult reading. Summarizes Rajalakshmi's research and recommendations for improving nutrition in India.

————, ed. *Nutrition and the Development of the Child*. Baroda, India: University of Baroda, 1982. Papers given at conference on nutrition. Difficult reading, but Rajalakshmi's opening and closing remarks and accounts of her research are interesting.

Richter, Derek, ed. *Women Scientists: The Road to Liberation*. London: Macmillan, 1982. Chapter by Rajalakshmi recalls her life and summarizes her research.

Lydia Makhubu showed that plants used as medicines by traditional African healers can have powerful effects on the body. (Courtesy University of Swaziland)

Lydia Phindile Makhubu

(1937–)

For weeks, a woman has been having stomach pains that no one can explain. Her family may take her to a doctor at a hospital clinic. But in many parts of Africa, they are also likely to ask a traditional healer for help.

The healer will talk to family members about the woman's problem, just as a Western doctor would. But he or she may also go into a trance to consult spirits or use animal bones as a divining tool. The healer will then recommend a treatment, most often a mixture of several plants. The medicine may be rubbed into cuts in the skin, burned and breathed as smoke, or swallowed in water.

Such procedures may seem foolish to people used to Western medicine. Chemist Lydia Makhubu, however, has shown that plants used by traditional African healers can have powerful effects on the body. Used in the right way, they may well cure illness.

Analyzing medicinal plants is only one of the things Makhubu has done to try to bring traditional culture and modern science together. She has done much to improve science education and advance the role of women scientists in Africa.

Lydia Phindile Makhubu was born on July 1, 1937, at the Usuthu Mission in Swaziland. Swaziland, a country about the size of New Jersey, is just east of South Africa. For many years the British controlled its government, but it became independent in 1968. It is currently ruled by a king.

Lydia's father was a teacher, but he also worked in the mines of South Africa for a while. He was trained as a medical technician while in South Africa. When he returned to Swaziland, he worked as an assistant in health clinics. Lydia grew up in the clinics.

Lydia Makhubu can't recall how she became interested in science, but that interest was well established by the time she went to Pius XII College in Lesotho, a nearby south African country. She studied both mathematics and chemistry. Organic chemistry, the study of complex carbon-containing compounds usually found in living things, interested her the most. She graduated in 1963.

Makhubu won a Canadian Commonwealth Scholarship, which allowed her to study for a master's degree at the University of Alberta in Edmonton. She wanted to know how drugs or medicines work in the body, so she studied pharmacy as well as organic chemistry. She received her master's degree in 1967. She then went on to the University of Toronto, from which she obtained a Ph.D. in medicinal chemistry in 1973. She was the first Swazi woman ever to earn a Ph.D. degree.

After completing her education, Makhubu returned to her home country and joined the faculty of the University of Swaziland. She has been there ever since. She became a full professor of chemistry in 1980.

During the 1970s, in addition to keeping up a heavy teaching schedule, Makhubu carried out research on plants used in traditional Swazi medicine. She began by collecting plants that healers used as medicines and listing the ailments the plants were supposed to cure. Using a grant from the

World Health Organization, she even paid a healer to make up plant medicines at the university. Because testing equipment was limited in Swaziland, she sent the medicines to the United States to be analyzed. The analyses showed that most of the plants contained chemicals that can have powerful effects on the body.

Makhubu felt that studying traditional plant medicines was important for several reasons. First, such studies might lead to the recognition of medicines that could be used in other parts of the world. Work such as hers also preserved information that had been handed down only by word of mouth and was being lost as the country's culture changed.

Most important, Makhubu has pointed out, many people in Swaziland still go to traditional healers. "For this reason I think it is extremely important that this system of medicine should be elevated and standardized so that it . . . serves them properly," she told a Voice of America interviewer in 1980. For example, scientific analysis can help healers work out the best dosage, or amount, of medicine to be taken. Makhubu feels that traditional healers can work well with modern doctors if both groups show respect and understanding.

In the 1980s, Makhubu's research became focused on an African plant called *Phytolacca dodecandra*, or endod. This plant poisons water-dwelling snails that carry a worm parasite. The parasite causes a serious human disease called schistosomiasis, or

In my opinion, the major reason for the survival of the traditional system [of African medicine] in spite of the modern ways of life, is its approach. It is a wholistic system utilizing [using] treatment which focuses not only on symptoms [signs of illness] but also on psychological and sociological factors.

—Lydia Makhubu

"snail fever." The worms leave the snails, swim free in rivers and streams, and burrow into the body of anyone who drinks or swims in the water. They damage lungs, liver, and other organs. In some parts of Africa and Asia, schistosomiasis is the most widespread disease and leading cause of death. Because the worms must spend part of their lives in snails, killing the snails is an effective way of stopping the spread of the disease. Endod may be cheaper than Western snail poisons.

While Makhubu was carrying out her research, she was also taking an ever-growing part in the administration of the University of Swaziland. She became dean of the science faculty in 1976 and pro-vice-chancellor in 1978. Since 1988 she has been the university's vice-chancellor. She is the first woman in southern Africa to hold such a high post. She also headed the Association of Commonwealth Universities in 1989–90 and was the first woman to do so. In addition to her double career as researcher and university administrator, Makhubu has a full family life. She is married to Daniel Mbatha, a surgeon, and they have a son and a daughter.

Makhubu's main interests today, besides her work at the university, are furthering science education in Africa and encouraging women scientists in developing nations. Scientists, she points out, are needed to develop Swaziland's agriculture and industries. "I think science will be in future the most important thing for the development of Swaziland," she has said. And the key to getting more scientists, in turn, is developing science education. Improving science education in Swaziland, she says, is her chief ambition.

Makhubu has worked toward that ambition as president of the Royal Swaziland Society of Science and Technology, an organization she founded in 1977 and has headed ever since. In addition to helping to spread information among scientists, this organization tries to help ordinary people in Swaziland understand the importance of science. For example, it has produced radio programs that relate everyday subjects to science.

Makhubu says that she herself has never felt that being a woman held back her scientific career. She thinks this may be "because I never think of myself as a woman. I push ahead if I think I should push ahead." She recognizes, however, that many other women from developing nations who want to be scientists have had a more difficult time. Because of cultural pressures, few are able to go beyond a bachelor's degree before having to quit their jobs or studies and begin raising a family. Makhubu believes that the best way of producing more women scientists from these nations is to improve the quality of science education available to girls.

To encourage women from developing nations to advance in science, Makhubu helped to found the Third World Organization of Women in Science (TWOWS) in 1989. She was its first chairperson and has been its president since 1993. This organization presently has its headquarters in Trieste, Italy. Its main objective is to promote women in science and technology in developing nations and strengthen women's research activities. For example, it provides travel grants so that women scientists from developing nations can attend conferences and seminars in other countries. TWOWS has a membership of more than 1,000 women, of whom nearly 300 are from Africa.

Makhubu thinks women scientists can be particularly helpful in Africa's development because they

I'm very, very concerned about the appreciation of science, not only among those who had a formal education in science but the nation as a whole . . . because I think there is a very strong relationship between our everyday life and science.

—Lydia Makhubu

can combine science with women's traditional focus on family and society. They can "influenc[e the] scientific agenda to take into account social concerns and . . . influenc[e] society to embrace the positive aspects of science and technology." She notes, "Some of Africa's greatest concerns today include finding ways to increase food production, to manage natural resources and the environment, nutrition, improved health and education. These areas are in many ways related to those in which women have traditionally found their functions."

Makhubu has received many honors for her research and her work in furthering science education. She has received honorary degrees from Queen's University in Canada and from the Council for National Academic Awards in Britain, for example. She has won research grants from the European Economic Community, USAID, and the MacArthur Foundation. She has also served on international councils and committees, including the WHO Medical Research Council and the United Nations Advisory Committee on Science and Technology. She is vice president of the African Academy of Sciences.

The Voice of America said in 1980 that Lydia Makhubu "is making a unique contribution to the advancement of science, and to the progress of blacks and women in the world of the intellect in southern Africa." Her assistant, Anita Smith, adds that Makhubu "has made her mark in the academic and scientific world and yet remains a warm and unspoiled person."

Chronology

July 1, 1937	Lydia Makhubu born at Usuthu Mission, Swaziland
1963	graduates from Pius XII College, Lesotho
1967	receives master's degree from University of Alberta, Edmonton

1973	receives Ph.D. from University of Toronto; joins faculty of University of Swaziland
1970s	does research on plant medicines used by traditional Swazi healers
1976	becomes dean of science faculty
1977	founds Royal Swaziland Society of Science and Technology
1978	becomes pro-vice-chancellor
1980	becomes full professor of chemistry
1980s	does research on use of endod to kill parasite-bearing snails
1988	becomes vice-chancellor of University of Swaziland
1989	helps to found Third World Organization of Women in Science (TWOWS)
1989–90	becomes first woman to head Association of Commonwealth Universities
1993	becomes president of TWOWS

Further Reading

Aikman, Lonelle. *Nature's Healing Arts*. Washington, D.C.: National Geographic Society, 1977. Provides background information on plant medicines and other treatments used by traditional healers in many countries.

Makhubu, Lydia Phindile. *The Traditional Healer*. Kwaluseni, Swaziland: University of Botswana and Swaziland, 1978. Describes how traditional Swazi healers train for their work, discover the causes of illness, and treat it; lists some of the plants they use.

Science in Africa. Washington, D.C.: Voice of America, 1982. Includes an interesting interview with Makhubu; primary printed source of information on her.

Biruté Galdikas has spent her life studying the orangutan, one of humans'
closest animal relatives. (Courtesy Orangutan Foundation International; photo, Allan Altcheck)

Biruté M. F. Galdikas

(1946–)

W ho are we, really? What makes us human? And how did we come to be this way?

Some of the answers to these questions may lie in the behavior of red-haired apes called orangutans. This name, given to the animals by the human natives of the orangutans' homeland in Indonesia, means "people of the forest." Orangutans' lives and social relationships hint at what those of our human ancestors may have been like 15 million years ago, when those ancestors still lived in trees.

But time for studying wild orangutans may be running out. Half a million of them once ranged throughout southern Asia, but now they are found only on the islands of Borneo and Sumatra. There are estimated to be between 10,000 and 20,000 wild orangutans left today—and that number shrinks every year.

Most of what we know about orangutans has come from the studies of one woman, Biruté M. F. Galdikas. Galdikas has devoted her life to studying the "people of the forest" in their native home. She also works to preserve the animals and their habitat and tries to return captive orangutans to a normal life in the forest.

Biruté Galdikas is truly an international scientist. She has parents from one country, was born in a second, grew up in a third, studied in a fourth, and works in a fifth! Galdikas's parents, Filomena and Antanas Galdikas, came from the small country of Lithuania, in central Europe. When the Soviet Union took control of Lithuania at the end of World War II, Filomena and Antanas separately fled the country. They met in a refugee camp.

Biruté, the Galdikases' first child, was born on May 10, 1946, in Wiesbaden, Germany. Two years later the family moved to Canada, where Antanas Galdikas found work as a miner and Filomena as a nurse. Biruté spent most of her childhood in Toronto, Ontario. Two brothers and a sister eventually were added to her family.

As a child, Biruté loved to visit the zoo and watch the monkeys and apes. She knew that the great apes—chimpanzees, gorillas, and orangutans—are humans' closest living relatives. They shared an ancestor millions of years ago. Of the three, orangutans always interested Biruté the most.

Galdikas began attending the University of British Columbia in 1962. Her family moved to southern California three years later, and she transferred to the University of California at Los Angeles (UCLA). There she majored in anthropology, the study of human beings and their behavior. After graduation she remained at UCLA and began working toward a master's degree in the same subject. But what she really wanted to do was study orangutans.

Her chance came in 1969, when an anthropologist named Louis Leakey gave a talk at the university. Leakey shared Galdikas's belief that

I remember thinking that if we understood our closest human relatives we'd understand our origins . . . maybe our own behavior.

—Biruté Galdikas

much could be learned about early human society by making long-term studies of wild apes. Galdikas knew he had already sponsored two such studies, both by young women. An Englishwoman named Jane Goodall was observing chimpanzees in Tanzania, and an American, Dian Fossey, was doing the same for mountain gorillas in Rwanda, another African country. Leakey preferred to have women do studies of this kind because he believed they were more careful and patient observers than men were.

When Leakey's lecture was over, Galdikas introduced herself and told him about her interest in orangutans. She asked him to help her set up a study like those of Goodall and Fossey. "I knew, even before I went up to him . . . this was it," she said later.

Leakey didn't seem so sure. Before accepting Galdikas, he used a deck of cards to give her what he said was a memory test. While trying to remember which cards Leakey was turning over, Galdikas noticed that some cards were slightly bent. She mentioned this to Leakey, and he told her she had passed the test. Most men, he said, never noticed this seemingly unimportant detail. Yet it was exactly such details, he believed, that were likely to prove the most important to science. After further discussion, he agreed to help her.

Even with Leakey behind her, it took two years to find funding for Galdikas's project. (Leakey himself was not wealthy.) But at last, in September 1971, she reached Indonesia.

She did not go alone. While in college, Galdikas had met a Canadian student in physics and computer science named Rod Brindamour. They married in 1969, the same year Galdikas received her master's degree. Brindamour was not as fascinated by orangutans as Galdikas, but he agreed to go to Indonesia with her.

Galdikas and Brindamour had planned to work in the well-mapped Mount Looser Reserve in Sumatra, where some earlier orangutan studies had been done. The head of Indonesian parks and nature reserves, however, told them to go to Tanjung Puting, on the south coast of Borneo. This wilder nature reserve had never been fully explored.

The young couple arrived in Tanjung Puting with only the supplies they could cram into two backpacks: four sets of clothes, cameras, notebooks, two raincapes, a small amount of cooking and scientific equipment, and one flashlight. Their camp consisted of a bug-infested hut with bark walls and a roof of thatch (woven vegetation). They named it Camp Leakey.

The forest did not make them welcome. The temperature averaged 90° Fahrenheit, and the humidity was almost 100 percent. Constant dampness made their clothes rot. When the pair staggered back to camp, exhausted, at the end of each day, Galdikas wrote later, "fat black leeches, bloated with our blood, dropped out of our socks and off our necks and fell out of our underwear." Nonetheless, Galdikas loved the rain forest. She has called it "a great cathedral."

Each morning, Brindamour headed away from camp in one direction to clear trails. Galdikas went in another direction, looking for orangutans. Usually she didn't find any. Living high in the trees, the fruit-eating apes were hard to spot. Galdikas more often heard them, or rather the small branches and fruit seeds they dropped, than saw them. If they saw her first, they shrieked and threw down larger branches before moving quickly away.

Galdikas had been in the forest two months before she was able to track a single animal for a whole day. She followed a mother and her youngster until nightfall, when the mother made a sleeping nest of leaves among the tree branches. Next morning, while it was still dark, Galdikas and Brindamour went back to the tree and waited. The leaf nest finally began to shake, and the mother and baby crawled out. The day, Galdikas remembered later, was Christmas Eve. "It was the best Christmas present I ever had," she said. They followed the mother and baby for five days. During that time the animals fed, traveled by swinging gracefully from branch to branch, and rested, but they did not meet a single other orangutan. This seemed to support other scientists' conclusion that orangutans lead a solitary life.

As the months wore on, the couple met and followed other orangutans. They learned to recognize individuals by features such as scars or broken fingers. As Goodall and Fossey also did, they named the animals. When they knew or suspected that two animals were related, they gave them names beginning with the same letter of the alphabet. The first mother and baby they followed, for instance, they called Beth and Bert.

The orangutans, in turn, slowly became habituated, or used to the presence of humans. Once they learned that Brindamour and Galdikas offered no threat, the apes stopped throwing branches at them and simply ignored them.

Three years was the longest time any other scientist had studied orangutans in the wild. Galdikas and Brindamour stayed four years before even taking a break. By then they had spent 6,804 hours watching a total of 58 orangutans that they could recognize and name.

The two confirmed that, except for mothers and babies, orangutans spend very little time interacting with each other. In this they are different from chimpanzees and gorillas, which live and travel in groups. The difference probably arises from the fact that orangutans eat mostly fruit, which is widely scattered through the forest. This food supply is not large enough to support several animals that stay together.

Even so, Galdikas learned that orangutans were not quite as solitary as they seemed. Two or three adolescent, or subadult, females (those four years old or more) often traveled together for several days, for example. They ate together and sometimes groomed each other.

Only adult male orangutans lived almost completely alone. Just one mature male lived in each territory. He spent time with another orangutan only when a female was ready to mate.

If another adult male approached while a male and female were together, the two males would fight. With burly 300-pound bodies (twice the size of females) and faces swollen by fleshy cheek pads, the males looked like the fearsome wrestlers they were.

Most orangutan battles occurred in the trees. Sometimes the warriors fell many feet to the ground, then chased each other back up to begin the fight again. As they fought, the males gave their long calls, which Galdikas described as "a hair-raising, minutes-long sequence of roars and groans that can carry a mile." When a male made his long call, a pouch of skin under his throat swelled impressively.

As if tracking wild orangutans were not enough, Galdikas at the same time was being "mother" to a hutful of orphaned orangutan babies. She had gotten into the orangutan-mothering business almost as soon as she set up camp. Government officials asked her and Brindamour to create a "halfway house" where baby orangutans taken from captivity could be cared for and prepared to return to life in the forest. The babies usually had been taken by poachers and sold as pets.

Galdikas's first orangutan baby was one-year-old Sugito. Baby orangutans hold onto their mothers day and night for at least two years, and Sugito wanted to do the same with Galdikas. If she tried to set him down, he screamed and resisted so desperately that he caused bruises.

Sugito was followed by a steady stream of others. Galdikas usually cooked, washed, slept, or followed wild orangutans with one or more orphan babies clinging to her body.

Galdikas became "mother" to orphaned baby orangutans, which clung to her day and night. (Courtesy Orangutan Foundation International)

And when the babies grew up enough to release their hold, matters grew even worse. "Sometimes," Galdikas wrote, "I felt as though I were surrounded by wild, unruly children in orange suits who had not yet learned their manners." The babies tore up mattresses, ripped holes in the straw roof of the hut, and ate everything from candles to shampoo. "It was a continual battle of wits," Galdikas says ruefully, "and they won!" To get a little peace, Galdikas and Brindamour finally built themselves an orangutan-proof wooden house with screened windows. They were glad for more reasons than one when the youngsters were finally ready to leave camp.

Galdikas's life was further complicated on October 17, 1976, when she gave birth to her own child, Binti Paul. Binti grew up among the ex-captive orangutans in camp, and he often imitated their behavior.

In 1978, Galdikas wrote up all the observations she had made on wild orangutans so far. She submitted the result to UCLA as her Ph.D. paper. The scientists who saw the paper admired its many statistical tables, which were a contrast to the narrative style that Goodall and Fossey preferred. Many scientists felt that from a scientific point of view, Galdikas's work was the best of the three.

No matter how difficult life in Camp Leakey became, Galdikas had the satisfaction of knowing she was doing exactly what she wanted to do. The same was not true of Rod Brindamour. One day in 1979 he told Galdikas, "I'm 30. I don't have a car, a bank account or a degree. I don't have anything I can put on my resumé except seven and a half years in the jungles of Borneo." He said he wanted to return to his career in computer science. He also explained that he had fallen in love with Yuni, the young Indonesian woman who had been hired to help take care of Binti. They wanted to marry.

Brindamour returned to Canada in the middle of 1979, taking Yuni with him. Six months later, Galdikas reluctantly let Binti join them. She and Brindamour were both concerned that the boy was acting too much like an orangutan. Once in a conventional home in Vancouver, Binti quickly gave up his orangutan ways.

Galdikas, meanwhile, found another partner who was more sympathetic to her work. His name was Pak Bohap bin Jalan. A member of the Dayak tribe, he was one of the Indonesian workers Galdikas had hired as the camp grew larger. She and Bohap married in 1981 and later had two children, Frederick and Jane. Unlike Binti, Frederick and Jane grew up with human as well as orangutan playmates because Indonesian workers' families lived in or near the camp.

Today, most support for Galdikas's work comes from a nonprofit organization she started in 1986, the Orangutan Foundation International. The organization's headquarters are in Los Angeles, but it has branch offices in Australia, Canada, England, Indonesia, and Taiwan. Its purpose is to raise money for programs to preserve, study, and educate people about orangutans and their forest home.

Galdikas still spends most of the year at Camp Leakey. She continues both her studies of wild orangutans and her rehabilitation of ex-captive babies. She says her most important recent observation on wild orangutans is the discovery of how often females give birth. Female orangutans in zoos have a baby about every four years. Galdikas found, that the average time between babies among wild orangutans is twice as long. This low birth rate may add to the survival problems of the species.

Galdikas has now returned more than 80 ex-captive orangutans to the forest. In addition to helping these individuals, she says, the rehabilitation program serves a second purpose: increasing direct contact between people and orangutans. It is impossible for visitors to have contact with wild orangutans, she says, because the apes are "150 feet up in the top of a tree." But the friendly, curious ex-captives are a different matter. Galdikas recalls the time an important Indonesian official visited the camp. "An orangutan female hugged him! . . . He was utterly thrilled."

My main contribution [to science] is staying in one place, following one population longer than anyone.

—Biruté Galdikas

With contact comes understanding and sympathy. "The rehabilitation programs have really focused the attention of the local people [and] the local government on the importance of orangutans and . . . the tropical rain forest habitat," Galdikas says. Such support is vital because destruction of the rain forest for logging, farmland, and other purposes is by far the greatest threat to wild orangutans' survival. Such destruction can be stopped only if local people want it to be.

For the same reason, Galdikas welcomes tourists to her camp. They are brought in groups to watch the afternoon feeding of the ex-captives. Galdikas notes proudly that thousands of people from all over the world have visited Camp Leakey. Once they have had contact with orangutans, she says, "people start paying attention to them. And once they pay attention to orangutans, they also have to pay attention to the tropical rain forest, which is their only home."

Chronology

May 10, 1946	Biruté Galdikas born in Wiesbaden, Germany
1962	enters University of British Columbia
1965	transfers to UCLA
1969	meets Louis Leakey; receives master's degree; marries Rod Brindamour
September 1971	Galdikas and Brindamour reach Indonesia
fall 1971	set up Camp Leakey; begin following wild orangutans and caring for ex-captive baby orangutans
December 24, 1971	Galdikas succeeds in following a single orangutan for a whole day
1978	receives Ph.D. from UCLA for research on wild orangutans

1979	Brindamour returns to Canada, divorces Galdikas
1981	Galdikas marries Pak Bohap bin Jalan
1986	establishes Orangutan Foundation International

Further Reading

Galdikas, Biruté M. F. "Living with the Great Orange Apes." *National Geographic*, June 1980. Lively account of Galdikas's experiences with orangutans in the 1970s.

———. *Reflections of Eden: My Years with the Orangutans of Borneo*. Boston: Little, Brown, 1994. Galdikas's recent book describes her life with orangutans.

Galdikas-Brindamour, Biruté. "Orangutans, Indonesia's 'People of the Forest.'" *National Geographic*, October 1975. Describes Galdikas and Brindamour's first experiences with orangutans in Indonesia.

Gallardo, Evelyn. *Among the Orangutans: The Biruté Galdikas Story*. San Francisco: Chronicle Books, 1993. Book for young people, done with Galdikas's cooperation, describes her life and work.

Kevles, Bettyann. *Watching the Wild Apes*. New York: Dutton, 1976. Book for young adults describes the early research of Galdikas, Goodall, and Fossey.

Lessem, Don. "Interview: Biruté Galdikas." *Omni*, July 1987. Interesting interview describes Galdikas's life and career.

Montgomery, Sy. *Walking with the Great Apes*. Boston: Houghton Mifflin, 1991. Describes lives and work of Biruté Galdikas, Jane Goodall, and Dian Fossey.

Starowicz, Mark. "Leakey's Last Angel." *New York Times Magazine*, August 16, 1992. Long article includes relatively recent information on Galdikas, including problems with the Indonesian government that Galdikas says have since been solved.

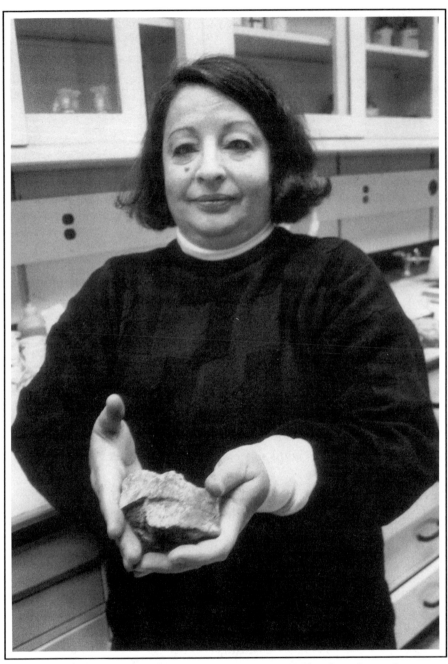

Aslihan Yener's discovery of an ancient tin mine in Turkey has changed scientists' understanding of the long-ago period called the Bronze Age. (Courtesy Oriental Institute, University of Chicago)

Kutlu Aslihan Yener
(1946–)

Nearly 5,000 years ago, in a land called Anatolia (now part of Turkey), children 12 to 15 years old wearily climbed a mountain each morning. They entered dark tunnels almost too narrow for adults to pass. Deep inside the mountain, the young miners lit fires against rock walls to soften the ore, or metal-bearing mineral. Then they pounded the ore free with stone tools.

Aslihan Yener paints this gloomy scene as she describes her discoveries inside a hill called Kestel, in the Taurus Mountains. But her findings in the mine of Kestel and in the ruins of a nearby ore-refining town do more than reveal a sad example of child labor. They rewrite history.

Between about 3000 and 1100 B.C., most metal objects, from swords to hair ornaments, were made of bronze. Bronze is an alloy, or mixture, of metals composed of tin and copper. Bronze was so important to civilizations of the Near East, which were among the most highly developed peoples in the world at the time, that this period is called the Bronze Age.

Copper was common in the Near East, but tin was not. Ancient writings of the Assyrians, a people who lived in what is now Syria and northern Iraq, claimed that they brought all the area's tin from the east, perhaps from the Hindu Kush (now Afghanistan), a thousand miles away. Yener, however, says that the mine at Kestel produced a significant amount of tin. The discovery that some Bronze Age tin could have come from the Near East itself changes scientists' understanding of the trading in this period, when complex civilizations and international trade were just starting to appear.

It does not seem surprising that Aslihan Yener is interested in Anatolian history, since she comes from Turkey. She was born in Istanbul on July 21, 1946. She was raised in the United States, however. Her businessman father, Reha Turkkan, and her mother, Emire Guntekin, brought their family to New Rochelle, New York, when Aslihan was only six months old. They also have a second daughter, Jaylan.

Aslihan's liking for science began early. "I almost lived at the Natural History Museum in New York," she says. She also had excellent high school science classes, thanks partly to the push for better science education that occurred in the United States in the late 1950s. "It was the right time and the right place."

In 1964, when Aslihan entered Adelphi University in Garden City, New York, she planned to study chemistry. Like Lise Meitner, she was "interested in the fundamental blocks that make up the world." After a few years, however, she "got the travel bug" and went to Turkey. She transferred to Robert College (now Bosphorus University) in Istanbul in 1966.

At first Yener studied art history, examining the Roman ruins along Turkey's coast. But she soon discovered that the traces of earlier cultures buried under the classical ruins interested her even more. She therefore changed her major to archaeology, the study of the physical remains of ancient civilizations. After her graduation in 1969, she continued this new interest at Columbia University in New York. She studied at Columbia from 1972 to 1980, when she received a Ph.D.

As her first major archaeology project, Yener used chemical techniques to trace the origins of silver in objects made by ancient Near Eastern civilizations. She found that some of the silver came from mines in the Taurus Mountains. In Bronze Age times, these mountains were part of an area called Anatolia. Indeed, Yener discovered, mining in the Taurus Mountains had been more extensive than anyone had dreamed.

Yener next became interested in tin, which was even more important to ancient Near Eastern civilizations than silver because it was both scarce and essential for making bronze. She says tin was as valuable a resource in Bronze Age times as oil is today.

In 1982, while Yener was an associate professor in history at Bosphorus University (a post she held from 1980 to 1988), she found traces of tin in some of the Taurus Mountains mines. This surprised her because records left by the Assyrians, an ancient trading people who lived south and east of Anatolia, had claimed that they were importing tin to Anatolia. This suggested that there was no important source of tin in the Near East at the time. Yener began to wonder whether the Assyrians might have been reluctant to mention a source of tin that could have competed with the tin they brought from a distant eastern source such as the Hindu Kush—especially since the source was close by and its tin probably was cheaper.

But finding traces of tin was not the same as finding a tin mine. For

In one six-square-mile area, where I thought there might be 30 or 40 mines, we found 850.

—Aslihan Yener, on mining in the Taurus Mountains

five years, Yener and her coworkers in the Turkish Geological Research and Survey Directorate looked for a Bronze Age mine that contained good enough tin ore to suggest that tin had really been taken regularly from that spot. Their search was unsuccessful.

Then one day in the summer of 1987, another scientist in the geological survey called Yener in Istanbul. In sand and silt from a stream in the Taurus foothills, he said, he had found reddish-purple crystals with a glassy shine. Tests showed that the crystals were cassiterite, a kind of tin ore. Since he knew Yener was interested in tin, he wanted her to know about his find.

This news excited Yener tremendously. Most tin ores are black, so she and the others had been looking for black minerals. They could have walked right by this unusual purple substance without recognizing it. She left immediately to see the spot her friend had described, making the 15-hour drive without stopping.

Not far from this site, in a deserted valley, Yener found the mine she had been searching for. It was inside a hill that local people called Kestel. Fragments of Bronze Age pottery in and near the mine suggested that the mine had been used in those ancient times. And inside the mine itself, Yener saw veins of wine-colored cassiterite ore.

Ever since then, Yener and her archaeological team have been exploring this mine. Between 1990 and 1993 her work was supported by the National Endowment for the Humanities, the National Geographic Society, and the Smithsonian Institution. Since that time she has been sponsored by the Oriental Institute of the University of Chicago, where she is an assistant professor.

The team has found that the Kestel mine contains about two miles of damp, muddy tunnels. Many are only about two feet wide—a fact that offered the first hint that children had done the mining. "I slid down into one of the shafts with a rope tied around my waist. It was one of the scariest things I've ever done in my life," Yener says. The researchers later found a burial site in an abandoned mine shaft that contained several skeletons of children aged 12 to 15. The young workers probably died in the mine and were buried there. (Many cultures have used child labor, including child miners, until fairly recent times.)

To prove that tin had been mined at Kestel, Yener needed to find a nearby site where the metal was extracted from the mine's ore. She found a possible site just as her 1989 excavation season was about to end. Some of her students, exploring a hill opposite the Kestel mine, discovered piles of Bronze Age pottery such as workers might have used. When Yener joined them, she found a large collection of stone tools as well—50,000 of them in an area just half a mile across.

Yener believes that this hill, now called Goltepe, once held what was for its time a good-sized city. Up to a thousand people may have lived and worked there. Much of the city was built into or even under the ground, with workshops and houses carved into the bedrock. Dating of objects found at Goltepe shows that the city was occupied more or less continuously between 3290 and 1840 B.C.

Some of the pottery found at Goltepe has provided the proof Yener needed that the city was really devoted to refining tin. The fragments had once been part of thick bowls called crucibles. They were covered with a glassy material that she recognized as slag, the part of ore that is left after most of the metal in the ore has been extracted. Yener had some of the slag analyzed at the Smithsonian Institution to find out what elements it contained. The results of the test were shown on a computer-produced graph, and "when the tin peaks came shooting up on the graph, we started dancing up and down and hugging each other," Yener recalls. Most of the slag contained at least 30 percent tin, enough to show

Yener believes that tin ore was ground up and heated in pottery crucibles to separate out the metal. (Courtesy Oriental Institute, University of Chicago)

that the ore had been a useful source of the metal. Some of the material on the crucible fragments was almost pure tin.

Combining her findings with what she and other scientists know of Bronze Age metalworking, Yener thinks she has figured out how the crucibles were used. Most likely, she says, the workers at Goltepe first washed nuggets of relatively pure tin out of the ore from the Kestel mine. They then used stone tools to pound the nuggets into powder. They put the powder in the thick pottery crucibles and covered it with burning charcoal. They probably made their fires hotter by blowing on the charcoal through reeds, as Egyptian metalworkers of the time were known to do. As the powder melted, the tin in it would have formed separate droplets of pure metal. These could be freed from the slag by pounding after the mixture cooled. This refining method would have required many workers, but it allowed tin to be recovered from relatively low-grade ores, at low temperatures, and with only the simplest tools.

As excavation at Kestel and Goltepe has continued, Yener has discovered even more. In the summer of 1993 she found proof that the Goltepe area was a major industrial site, disproving the common belief that the "high-tech" work of the era was done only in large cities. Furthermore, Yener says, her findings show that tin mining in Anatolia was "a fully developed industry with specialization of work" by 2870 B.C.—near the very beginning of the Bronze Age. Anatolia, in fact, may have been one of the birthplaces of Bronze Age metal technology.

Archaeologists still are not sure how important Anatolian tin was in the overall trading of Near Eastern Bronze Age civilizations. Most find

They were actually experimenting with metal technology . . . in the highlands and not down in the cities.

—Aslihan Yener

it hard to deny, however, that at least some tin could have come from this area. This means, Yener says, that marketers of tin from different sources would have had to compete against each other. That makes the picture of trading among these civilizations much more complex than had been thought. Vincent C. Pigott, an expert in the archaeology of metalworking at the University of Pennsylvania, says Yener's work is "excellent archaeology and a major step forward in understanding ancient metal technology."

Chronology

July 21, 1946	Kutlu Aslihan Yener born in Istanbul, Turkey
1964	enters Adelphi University
1966	transfers to Robert College in Istanbul
1969	graduates from Robert College
1972–80	studies at Columbia University
1980	receives Ph.D. from Columbia
1980–88	is associate professor at Bosphorus University
1982	finds traces of tin in mine in Taurus Mountains
1987	finds possible tin mine at Kestel
1989	finds metal-refining city at Goltepe
1993	joins Oriental Institute of University of Chicago; shows that Goltepe area was major industrial site

Further Reading

The Age of the God-Kings: TimeFrame 3000–1500 B.C. Alexandria, Va.: Time-Life Books, 1987. Provides background information on civilizations of the Bronze Age.

Bass, Thomas. "Land of Bronze." *Discover*, December 1991. Detailed popular description of Yener's life and work; most complete single source on Yener.

Wilford, John Noble. "Enduring Mystery Solved as Tin Is Found in Turkey." *New York Times*, January 4, 1994. Provides extensive update on Yener's research.

Index

Bold numbers indicate main headings.
Italic numbers indicate illustrations.

S

T

U